TREASURES
from the Ukrainian Steppes

This publication was produced with the financial support of the Museums Assistance Program of Canadian Heritage and the Investors Group.

Pointe-à-Callière
Montréal Museum of Archaeology and History
350 Place Royale
Old Montréal, Québec
H2Y 3Y5
Telephone: (514) 872-9150
Fax: (514) 872-9151

The Museum is subsidized by the Ville de Montréal.

Legal deposit
Bibliothèque nationale du Québec, 4th quarter 1998
National Library of Canada, 4th quarter 1998
ISBN 2-921718-16-2

Cette publication est disponible en français.

TREASURES
from the Ukrainian Steppes

Souvenir of an Exhibition

POINTE-À-CALLIÈRE

Montréal Museum of Archaeology and History

Credits and Acknowledgements

Treasures from the Ukrainian Steppes was organized by Francine Lelièvre and presented from October 7, 1998 to February 7, 1999, at Pointe-à-Callière, the Montréal Museum of Archaeology and History, in co-operation with the Institute of Archaeology, National Ukrainian Academy of Sciences, in Kiev.

Guest Curator for the exhibition
Michel Lambert

Scientific Advisors

Institute of Archaeology, National Ukrainian Academy of Sciences, Kiev
Professor Denis Kozak, Ukrainian Curator for the exhibition
Elena Fialko, author of the technical descriptions from the Institute and Secretary for the exhibition
Contributors to the technical descriptions: D. Y. Noujhii, L. V. Koulakovskaya, A. G. Kolesnikov,
M. Y. Videiko, V. V. Otrochtchenko, V. Y. Mourzine, S. V. Poline, G. L. Yevdokimov, A. I. Koubichev,
V. V. Krapivina, V. N. Zotsenko

Consulting archaeologist, Montréal
Jacques Y. Perreault, Centre for classical studies, Université de Montréal

The Museum thanks the Institute for the information provided on its collection. It also thanks
Véronique Schiltz for providing us with her works for use as references and for reviewing the exhibition texts.
The comments accompanying the photographs in this publication are based on those texts.

This publication was produced under the direction of Francine Lelièvre, director, Pointe-à-Callière,
Montréal Museum of Archaeology and History.

Co-ordination of content
Annick Poussart

Publishing
Plurimedia Communications
Consulting and co-ordination : Pierrette Gagné
Artistic direction : Dominic Duffaud

Authors
Elena Fialko
Denis Kozak
Michel Lambert
Francine Lelièvre
Annick Poussart
Véronique Schiltz
Piotr Tolochko
The excerpts from Herodotus' *Histories* are drawn from the translation by Aubrey de Sélincourt,
revised by John M. Marincola, Penguin Books, 1996.

Photographs
Michel Lambert (unless otherwise indicated)
The Museum thanks the Institute of Archaeology, National Ukrainian Academy of Sciences, for its kind
permission to reproduce the photographs taken in Kiev by Mr. Lambert.

Illustrations
Benoît Léonard, Lucie Gauthier, Dominic Duffaud

Translation
Andrei Pavlov, Russian-French
Terry Knowles and Pamela Ireland, French-English

Proofreading
Monique Cloutier

Printing
Transcontinental Impression

Table of Contents

From Kiev...

Professor Piotr P. Tolochko, Director
Institute of Archaeology, National Ukrainian Academy of Sciences

It gives me great pleasure to salute the opening of *Treasures from the Ukrainian Steppes*, the fruit of joint efforts by the Institute of Archaeology, National Ukrainian Academy of Sciences, in Kiev, and Pointe-à-Callière, the Montréal Museum of Archaeology and History. When Francine Lelièvre, Director of Pointe-à-Callière, first expressed a desire to bring archaeological antiquities from Ukraine to Canada, we were immediately excited by the possibilities.

As the Institute and the Museum set about selecting pieces, we were able to assemble an original collection with something representing nearly every one of the great periods in the ancient history of Ukraine. The collection includes a set of prehistoric musical instruments, the only one of its kind; magnificent pieces from the Tripolye culture, the first agricultural society in Ukraine; a Bronze-Age skull with features modelled in clay; gold and silver artifacts from the Scythians and Sarmatians; and statuettes from the ancient city-states north of the Black Sea. Most of the pieces are from digs conducted in recent decades.

I am delighted that for the first time such a representative collection is coming to Canada, a country with which Ukraine has long-standing cultural bonds. Indeed, this exhibition will give Canadians of Ukrainian origin an opportunity to see the history of our country in a new light.

I welcome all visitors to *Treasures from the Ukrainian Steppes* and, on behalf of the Institute, I would like to express our profound gratitude to Francine Lelièvre and all her colleagues and partners for everything they have done to make our shared dream come true.

Signing ceremony, in Kiev. Back row, left to right: Francine Lelièvre, Michel Lambert and Sergei D. Krizhitskii. Front, Piotr P. Tolochko.

... to Montréal

Francine Lelièvre, Director, Pointe-à-Callière
Montréal Museum of Archaeology and History

Since it opened in 1992, Pointe-à-Callière has endeavoured not only to bring its visitors to know and appreciate the Montréal of today and yesterday, but also to give Montrealers and other Canadians a chance to admire original material evidence of the world's archaeological heritage. *Treasures from the Ukrainian Steppes,* mounted in co-operation with the Institute of Archaeology, National Ukrainian Academy of Sciences, represents an exceptional leap forward in accomplishing this second part of our mission. For aside from the indisputable magnificence of the pieces presented and the fact that many of them are being displayed for the first time, these treasures invite visitors on a fascinating journey through the history and archaeology of the steppes.

Treasures… the word alone seems to whisper of ancient splendours. And the gold of the Scythians certainly lights up the exhibition. But out on the wild steppes, in the hands of prehistoric hunters, growers and herders and later of early nomads, every object possessed a value that lay in its utility and honesty, surpassing the intrinsic worth of the material from which it was made. Spearheads, amulets, harness trappings, bronze finials… for archaeologists, all these are the first and almost the only evidence of the lives and beliefs of these peoples who had no written language, and of their free yet harsh existence. Pointe-à-Callière wanted to put all these "treasures" of bone, clay, gold and marble, too—for the exhibition takes us all the way to ancient Olbia—in context in a setting that would not only display them to advantage but also allow them to speak to every visitor. This has always been one of the Museum's basic objectives in everything it does. We seek to bring the work of archaeologists to the public and illustrate the importance of their findings.

This exhibition and this publication could never have overcome the distances and linguistic barriers involved without the unwavering faith of Messrs Kryzhitskii and Tolochko, and the wholehearted co-operation of Professor Kozak and his team. I salute them all and extend my warmest appreciation. We also had the invaluable support of historian Véronique Schiltz, who was kind enough to provide us with her remarkable volumes on the Scythians and nomads of the steppes and to review the texts for the exhibition. My sincere thanks to her. My gratitude also goes to our Guest Curator, Michel Lambert, and the other tireless members of the production team, including Annick Poussart and Pierrette Gagné. Thank you one and all.

We offer the *Treasures from the Ukrainian Steppes* exhibition, and this souvenir publication, as a tribute and modest support for our Ukrainian colleagues, who continue to labour diligently, in often difficult conditions, to preserve the collective memory of humanity. For while it is important to bring the results of archaeological research to the public, the research itself must go on.

Ancient Treasures from the Ukrainian Steppes

By Elena Fialko and Denis Kozak
Institute of Archaeology, National Ukrainian Academy of Sciences

The pieces in the Treasures from the Ukrainian Steppes *exhibition illustrate the most important chapters in the ancient history of Ukraine. They tell us about the creativity and, to some extent, the lifestyles of the different forebears of present-day Ukrainians.*

Located in southeastern Europe, Ukraine holds a vital place in both the history and geography of the continent. While Ukrainian soil accounts for only slightly more than one-twentieth of the land mass of the continent, it has yielded more than half of all European antiquities. This impressive wealth of archaeological materials would appear to be closely linked to Ukraine's key position between Europe and Asia and to the combination of its various natural assets: a moderate climate, powerful rivers, fertile soil and an abundance of plant and animal life.

It is hardly surprising, then, that the first humans in eastern Europe appeared close to one million years ago in what is now Ukraine.

Hunting mammoths, tracking bison

During the last ice age, 20 to 14 thousand years ago, the natural conditions in what is now Ukraine fostered the development of two different primitive societies: people who hunted mammoths and others who depended on bison for their survival.

The mammoth hunters dwelled in a region of Europe inhabited by mammoths living in the periglacial areas—a tundra zone that extends to the middle Dniepr basin and, in the far northwestern corner of modern-day Ukraine, to the Volhynia region and the upper Vistula. The mammoth hunters organized group hunts, lying in wait for their victims in river valleys along the creatures' migration routes. They ate the mammoths' flesh and used the bones of these enormous animals to build their dwellings, which were up to 4 or 5 metres in diameter.

There would have been five or six dwellings in each community of mammoth hunters. Ukrainian archaeologists have discovered six of these villages or camps in the middle Dniepr basin. The pieces brought to light during digs at one of these sites, near the settlement of Mezine, in Chernigov province, are presented in the *Treasures from the Ukrainian Steppes* exhibition.

In southern Ukraine, in the steppe region north of the Black Sea, another population group hunted bison, which formed the basis of their diet. These hunters drove their prey into ravines, where they slaughtered them with spears. The exhibition displays some of these spearheads, found at the Amvrossievka camp, in Donetsk province. In fact, an enormous concentration of bones was discovered near this camp, possibly from no fewer than one thousand bison.

Tripolye farmers

In the fourth and third millenniums B.C., a Neolithic agricultural civilization appeared in Ukraine, in the form of a group of villages which in some places were actually proto-cities. The Tripolye culture is named after a village near Kiev, where material traces of it were first discovered. The Tripolye culture covered a vast territory of at least 200,000 km², extending from the Carpathian Mountains in Romania to the middle reaches of the Dniepr, concentrated in areas with fertile soil that they were able to work with picks. They lived in characteristic two-storey dwellings. Evidence of their material culture includes red-, black- and white-painted ceramics and various objects made of copper, bone, horn and stone. The anthropomorphic and zoomorphic figurines displayed in the exhibition are an especially interesting category of archaeological finds associated with the Tripolye culture.

Livestock herders

Pastoral groups also appeared. Unlike the farmers, though, they left neither dwellings, villages nor any true variety of crafts behind. This is likely because they spent most of their time moving about with their herds, and required only a few simple, utilitarian objects to meet their day-to-day needs.

For these herders had a different vision of the world, one in which everything was subordinated to the needs of their cattle, their main food source, beginning with the availability of fertile pastures. As an expression of their attempts to make this grazing land their own, these Indo-European herdsmen raised a new type of structure: kurgans, burial mounds that first appeared on the Ukrainian steppes in the 6th millennium B.C. This practice was a way of marking their territory, of calling on the dead to watch over the living, and it would continue on the steppes for thousands of years.

Cimmerians, Scythians, Sarmatians and the emergence of nomadism

Early in the 1st millennium B.C., a number of crucial events radically altered not only the appearance of the Ukrainian steppes but also the lifestyles of the people living there. The first groups of Indo-Iranian peoples began penetrating farther and farther into the steppes north of the Black Sea, after crossing the Caucasus and the lands bordering Asia. Sometimes pushing strongly forward, at other times retreating, only to advance again in powerful waves, aggressive hordes of nomads invaded and roamed throughout these fertile lands over a period spanning many centuries. They competed with the agricultural communities already established there, for the land was suited both to farming and grazing. These nomads were the Cimmerians, Scythians and Sarmatians.

The Cimmerians are the oldest people of eastern Europe whose name is known with certainty, thanks to written records. They are mentioned in various ancient literary sources, for example Homer's *Odyssey* and Herodotus' *Histories,* as well as in the cuneiform texts left behind by the Assyrians and Babylonians. Their culture arose in the 10th century B.C. and continued to flourish until the 7th century B.C. The intermingling of different ethnic groups and the heightened contact with neighbouring peoples led to far-reaching changes in economic and daily life. It was the Cimmerians who formed the first major group of nomad tribes in the south of eastern Europe.

The Cimmerians were primarily horsemen and warriors, or so the written sources and the designs appearing on their vessels tell us. This is borne out by archaeological discoveries in funeral complexes. The *Treasures from the Ukrainian Steppes* exhibition displays bone ornaments for a horse's headgear and a whip handle, for instance, as well as a two-edged bronze sword blade. The two bronze bracelets from a warrior's tomb are another fascinating example and, like the other pieces mentioned, are perfect illustrations of Cimmerian art, characterized by geometric designs in the form of separate or concentric circles, rosettes, spirals, meanders and lozenges, in very surprising combinations. Zoomorphic images are extremely rare in Cimmerian art; only one piece, a ritual axe of stag horn, shows a combination of zoomorphic and geometric motifs. It is included in the exhibition.

A new wave of nomads, from the East, rolled over the steppes in the 7th century B.C., submerging the Cimmerian culture and ushering in a new period in Ukrainian history. This phase, which clearly belonged to the Scythians, is rightly considered one of the most significant and memorable periods in the history of our country.

There is a good deal of written information on the Scythians, but the most complete and detailed description of the land and people is certainly the account given by Herodotus in Book 4 of his *Histories.* The author describes not only the historic events and legends linked with the advent of the Scythians and their sometimes bellicose relations with neighbours, but also the nomads' daily life, their rituals and their appearance.

The Scythians were excellent riders and unparalleled archers. They spent most of their days on horseback, either waging war, raiding or pillaging nearby tribes, or simply wandering the steppes with their herds of sheep and horses. Women and children travelled by wagon, and men on horseback. Their lives, dress and adornment were those of nomads, of course, as the pieces discovered in tombs clearly depict. A splendid array of such pieces is presented in this exhibition.

Bit by bit, the Scythians came to dominate neighbouring tribes of agricultural peoples and began levying tribute—taxes of the time—on the Greek colonies. In the end, they controlled the trade routes across the steppes. This inexorably led to the emergence of clear economic strata in Scythian society, as their tombs dazzlingly show.

This differentiation in terms of material wealth reached its peak in the 4th century B.C., and particularly in the latter half of the century. For it was at this time that the grandiose tombs of members of the Scythian aristocracy began appearing on the steppes next to the modest burial mounds of ordinary nomads. The bodies laid to rest in these tombs included princes and kings, in the Solokha, Chertomlyk, Oguz and other kurgans, and aristocrats, at Alexandropol, Gaymanova, Tolstaya, Vichnevaya, Babina, Soboleva, in the Kozel, Deyev, Melitopolski, Berdanski and Bratolubovsky kurgans and at many other sites.

Most of the precious gold, silver, bronze, bone and other pieces prized by the Scythians came from ancient workshops where they were generally made to order, to reflect the nomads' tastes and traditions. This exhibition presents the most significant and spectacular pieces discovered in recent decades, from the collection of the Institute of Archaeology, National Ukrainian Academy of Sciences. One of the most remarkable, which deserves special mention, is the replica of the Tolstaya Mogila pectoral—an uncontested masterpiece from an ancient goldsmith's workshop, in which scenes of daily life are combined with graceful plant motifs and depictions of savage animals. Two equally spectacular pieces were unearthed from the Bratolubovsky kurgan: a goblet bearing four rows of similar attack scenes, and a ritual vessel or *phiale* showing six heads of horses in harness.

The pieces of golden jewellery from the Oguz kurgan are of another style entirely: an earring in the shape of a sphinx, a number of necklaces with delicate pendants—all of them different, and all of them wonderfully graceful and tasteful. Indeed, the Scythian chieftains' passion for luxury extended to every aspect of their lives: head-dresses, robes, even shoes themselves were covered in gold plaques, not to mention the many pieces of jewellery and decorated vessels of various shapes for daily and ritual use. Gold and silver were even used to adorn warriors' weapons and horses' harnesses.

Scythia rose and, like other civilizations, eventually fell. Beginning in the early 3rd century B.C., Scythian "monuments" disappeared from the steppes, indicating the end of Greater Scythia. The exact causes of the decline are not yet certain. We do know, however, that in the late 3rd and early 2nd centuries B.C., Indo-Iranian nomad herders called Sarmatians appeared in the parts of modern-day Ukraine inhabited in those days by the Scythians.

Judging by the written sources and archaeological data available, the Sarmatians were much like their predecessors, in terms of their mores and customs, lifestyle and outlook. They, too, were nomads, and consequently were attached primarily to their horses and their weapons. Their tombs most often contain pieces of harnesses, weapons, dishes and jewellery, albeit more modest and simple than those left behind by the Scythians. And although they are few in number, the pieces of jewellery made of precious metals display a most original style.

Greek neighbours

While the southern Ukrainian steppes were reeling under wave after wave of nomad invasions, the Greeks were building and expanding settlements and cities on the shores of the Euxine Sea and the Meotida (the Black Sea and the Sea of Azov). Between the 7th and 5th centuries B.C., they erected the settlement of Berezan (near the present-day city of Ochakov), the cities of Olbia (near today's Nikolayev) and Tyras (near what is now Belgorod-Dnestrovsky), Chersonesus (close to present-day Sevastopol) and, on the shores of the Kerch Strait, the Kingdom of the Bosphorus, with Panticapaeum as its capital. The Greek colonies established on the edges of the nomad world acted as links between the civilizations on the steppes and those of the ancient Mediterranean. The exhibition includes absolutely magnificent examples of sculptures, terracotta figurines, archaic ceramics and various pieces illustrating daily life in these colonial cities on the Ukrainian coast of the Black Sea.

The context was well suited to trade, and the cultures gradually enriched each other, both spiritually and materially. But as the nomad Scythian state withered and disappeared, the Greek *polis* also stopped expanding and began to decline in turn.

Ukraine is rooted in the Rus of medieval Kiev, itself descended from the ancient ruins of Greater Scythia, particularly at the edges of the forest. Kievan Rus existed as a state for close to three hundred years, from the late 9th century to the 13th century, its economic, social and cultural development easily comparable with the countries of medieval Europe. Indeed, the strong Christian state long protected the West from fierce Eastern invaders. But Ukraine's unique geopolitical situation would continue to shape its remarkable and tragic history for centuries to come.

Snapshot of an Exhibition

Michel Lambert and Annick Poussart

An exhibition, and for that matter a publication, is often born of chance meetings and relationships based on common interests. This was the case for Treasures from the Ukrainian Steppes, *an exhibition that arose from the desire to share the stories told by a number of remarkable pieces.*

Following a meeting with Professor S.D. Kryzhitskii, Francine Lelièvre and Guest Curator Michel Lambert travelled to the Institute of Archaeology of the National Ukrainian Academy of Sciences in Kiev, where they discovered—as they had hoped— a magnificent and largely unknown collection of Scythian gold. At the same time, however, they found bone, clay, terracotta, marble, ceramic and other treasures. Given the extraordinary voyage back through time that these pieces promised, the initial concept expanded, as the Project Director, the Guest Curator and the Curator of the Institute, Denis Kozak, selected pieces and thought about how they could best be displayed.

When the two Montrealers returned home, a production team was formed and Michel Lambert and the other author of these lines began to pull together the information provided by Professor Kozak about the pieces. Two experts also agreed to assist the Montréal team, by contributing advice and reference works and reviewing the texts of the panels: Jacques Y. Perreault, archaeologist and Director of the Centre for classical studies at the Université de Montréal, and historian Véronique Schiltz, whose remarkable volumes on the Scythians were one of our primary sources of information and inspiration. Finally, the dream could never have become a reality without the assistance of an eloquent narrator from ancient times, the Greek historian Herodotus (see inset).

Roger-Viollet

Herodotus (c. 484-425 B.C.)

It would be almost inconceivable to present an exhibition of Scythian treasures without the "Father of History," as he was dubbed by Cicero. For the fourth book of Herodotus' *Histories* relates captivating first-hand accounts of the daily lives and ancient customs of these nomads—accounts whose remarkable accuracy would be confirmed by archaeological digs some 2,400 years later.

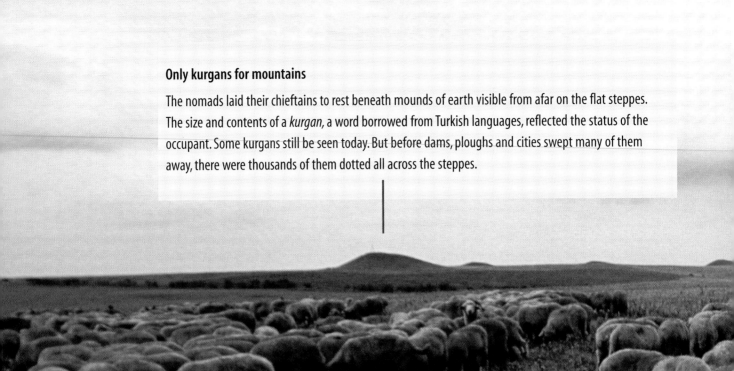

Only kurgans for mountains

The nomads laid their chieftains to rest beneath mounds of earth visible from afar on the flat steppes. The size and contents of a *kurgan,* a word borrowed from Turkish languages, reflected the status of the occupant. Some kurgans still be seen today. But before dams, ploughs and cities swept many of them away, there were thousands of them dotted all across the steppes.

Sisse Brimberg/National Geographic Image Collection

The treasures offered up for visitors' admiration evoke experiences, cultures and lifestyles far removed from our own. They tell of nomads' funeral rites and their taste for rich adornment. They depict the primordial role of horses in the turbulent destiny of the steppes and in day-to-day life. They attest to the artistic and commercial contacts between sedentary Greeks and nomad "barbarians." And we wanted this environment, this life in constant motion, all of this detail, to serve as a backdrop for the treasures. With the help of the graphic design firm, the setting for the exhibition is inspired by the natural environment of the steppes and the treasures displayed. It is divided into three zones, laid out chronologically and examining the subject matter through different themes.

Surroundings that reflect the immensity of the steppes

The pieces displayed were mostly discovered beneath the steppes of modern-day Ukraine or at the sites of ancient Greek colonies on the edges of the steppes. The first things visitors see when they enter the exhibition are a map and this photograph, to help them situate themselves geographically and grasp the immensity of the natural setting.

Like the curved lines of Scythian art and the ceaseless roaming of the nomads of the steppes, the exhibition leads visitors on a sinuous route, sometimes obliging them to retrace their steps. The zones are divided by tall semi-transparent cloth panels, helping to maintain as horizontal a feeling as possible in the room.

A chronological and thematic route

The pieces chosen date from 20,000 years B.C. to approximately 300 A.D., with the most recent ones from as late as the 12th century. To help visitors comprehend the stages in this long voyage, the exhibits and commentary are broken up into three zones: prehistory, the nomad invaders, particularly the Scythians, and finally the Greek colonies established around the same time on the northern shores of the Black Sea.

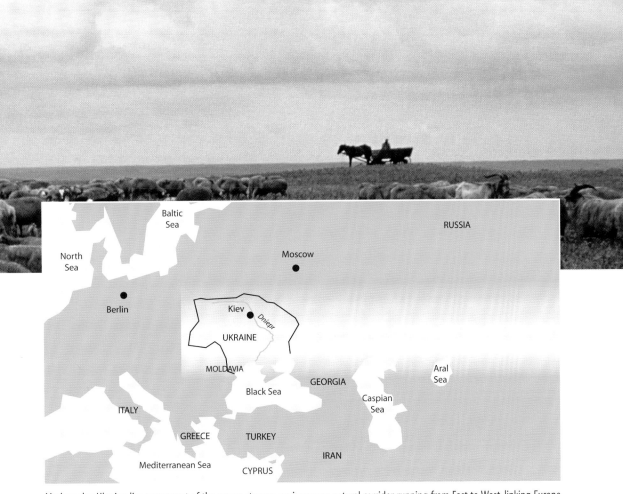

Modern-day Ukraine lies across part of the grassy steppes, an immense natural corridor running from East to West, linking Europe and Asia. Many tribes of nomad horsemen came this way seeking grazing land and water or to conquer new pastures.

The thunder of charging horsemen

Of course there was no way to exhibit all these pieces without paying tribute to the horse: the nomad's faithful companion in peace and war, buried alongside its master and adorned, like him, in its finest raiment. Indeed, the oldest traces ever found of the taming of horses are from southern Ukraine. One panel explains how the conquest of the horse was a decisive step in the emergence of nomadism. From time to time, on a long mural illustrating the expanse of the steppes, the magic of audiovisual technology brings to life the fearsome charges of phantom horsemen. And the visual signature of the exhibition, gracing pages 6 and 7 of this publication and inviting Montrealers to discover these treasures from the Ukrainian steppes, is quite naturally… a herd of galloping horses.

To find out more about the art of the steppes and nomad horsemen

An admirable work by Véronique Schiltz, *Les Scythes et les nomades des steppes* (L'Univers des formes, Gallimard).

The heart of the exhibition: the splendours of Scythian gold

Ritual vessels and *rhytons* testifying to the Scythians' fondness for Greek wine. Finery worn by warriors, princesses, children and horses. Ornamental plaques bearing the silhouette of a goddess or a galloping stag. Reconstructions of richly decorated head-dresses and shoes. At the heart of the exhibition, Scythian gold sparkles and glows, while a replica of a master-piece of Greco-Scythian art is displayed and explained in a neighbouring alcove (see inset).

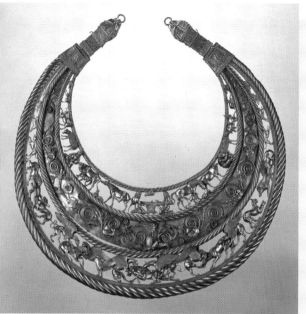

V. Terebenine / Ukraine Historic Treasures Museum

**View of original pectoral
(not included in the exhibition)**

Tolstaya Mogila site, town of Ordzhonikidze,
Dniepropetrovsk province (1971)
4th century B.C.
Gold

The replica of the Tolstaya Mogila pectoral

A depiction of the nomads' day-to-day lives and beliefs

The Institute's replica of this masterpiece is a veritable picture book of Scythian culture. The **topmost level** shows peaceful scenes from daily life. Two Scythians in horsemen's garb are working on a sheepskin coat. They wear hide trousers and soft leather boots—no need for rigid soles for riding on horseback without stirrups, nor for walking on grass or the soft carpets lining their wagons. Nearby are their *goryti,* quivers holding both the bow and arrows. The gracefully curving, flowering acanthus on the **middle level** seems to express the continuity between death and birth, like a tree linking heaven and earth. Death reigns on the **lower level**. Scythian art often showed scenes depicting a stag or horse being attacked by a griffin or panther. The pectoral shows more than forty animals, both real and imaginary. The horse, the nomad's companion in war and on his journeys, naturally has pride of place.

Situating visitors in time
At the entrance to each exhibition zone is an illustrated time line.

In the Stone Age
Objects of bone and ivory, dating from some 20,000 years ago

In the Bronze Age
Objects discovered in kurgans, evidence of a revolutionary alloy

In the time of the Tripolye people
Terracotta items left behind by Ukraine's great Neolithic civilization

Terrible funeral rites

Beneath the kurgan, adorned with gold, the embalmed corpse of the king lay in the main chamber, with his head facing east. Nearby lay a dagger or a sword, household articles and provisions for the beyond: amphorae full of wine, a cauldron containing the hind-quarters of a sheep. Other chambers contained the bodies of men and women, both nobles and servants, who had followed their master into the next world. At the top, a stone statue, or *baba*, stood guard over the primary tomb. Horses were also slaughtered and buried—sometimes more than a hundred of them!

To better illustrate the context in which the treasures of the Eurasian steppes were found, a model (not to scale) in the centre of the display cases of Scythian gold illustrates some characteristics of a rich kurgan, accompanied by short excerpts from Herodotus describing funeral rites (see inset).

Gregory Manchess/National Geographic Image Collection

The funeral rites of kings

When a king dies, […] they take up the corpse. […] it is carried in a waggon to a neighbouring tribe within the Scythian dominions, and then on to another. The people who successively receive it […] cut a piece from their ears, shave their hair […]. On each stage of the journey those who have already been visited join the procession.

Herodotus, *Histories,* Book IV

The Iron Age saw the emergence of nomadism and the first waves in a long series of invasions. This succession is shown by three display cases containing objects from the Cimmerian, Scythian and Sarmatian eras, respectively.

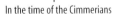

In the time of the Scythians
In the 7th century B.C., the Cimmerians were driven out by the Scythians, described by the Greek historian Herodotus as "nomads from Asia." For five centuries, the Scythians held sway over the lands north of the Black Sea.

On the shores of the Black Sea
Pieces of terracotta, glass and marble, evidence of Greek colonies on the edges of the steppes.

In the time of the Cimmerians
In the 9th century B.C., the Cimmerians thundered down on the lands to the north of the Black Sea. These are the first nomadic horsemen recorded in history, and their name is synonymous with destruction and pillage.

In the time of the Sarmatians
In the 2nd century B.C., the Scythians were supplanted by another group of nomads, the Sarmatians. Like the Scythians themselves, the Sarmatians' primary occupation was war. And like the Scythians, they too would eventually be conquered.

The gold pieces presented include small plaques that would have adorned nomads' clothing and belongings. This photograph of the skeleton of a rich Scythian woman discovered, along with the pectoral mentioned above, in the Tolstaya Mogila kurgan, shows the challenge facing archaeologists when they try to reconstitute the exact arrangement of such plaques on fabric that has long since crumbled to dust. The circular object is a bronze mirror.

Sisse Brimberg/National Geographic Image Collection

Herodotus tells of other rites that shock our modern sensitivities (and doubtless startled the Greeks of the time as well, with their different mores), along with many other "stories" relating to Scythians' beliefs, customs, strategies, daily lives and legends. His flowing, factual and yet always entertaining style keeps the reader turning the pages. The excerpts cited and the short summaries accompanying the pieces from the Institute will perhaps—or so we hope—encourage our readers to enjoy for themselves the entire spellbinding account.

Introducing visitors to a fascinating field of archaeology

One of the panels near the model kurgan gives a brief account of the archaeology of the steppes. The Museum also hopes to interest visitors in this remarkable subject.

Echoing the voices of gods and goddesses

The third and last exhibition zone presents figurines and statues that tell of the Greek presence on the shores of the Black Sea, on the fringes of the steppes. Some of the myths associated with these gods and goddesses, such as the adventures of Demeter and her daughter Persephone, have special relevance for Montrealers—who are certainly familiar with the rigours of winter!

And waves of invasions to come

To conclude the tour, a painted mural showing horsemen brandishing their weapons evokes the tumultuous centuries to come in the history of the Ukrainian steppes and leads to the end of the exhibition: two clay eggs, forerunners of today's coloured Easter eggs and symbolic of the birth of an independent Ukraine.

But we mustn't get ahead of ourselves! The following selection from the Institute's collection, with the exception of the Sarmatian period, invites you to plunge into the past of the steppes and Ukraine, starting in the Stone Age, when History was still Prehistory.

Enjoy your journey!

If you would like to read more of Herodotus…

Herodotus, *The Histories,* translated by Aubrey de Sélincourt, revised by John M. Marincola. Penguin Books.

Or to know more about the history and archaeology of the steppes…

Histoires de kourganes, La redécouverte de l'or des Scythes, by Véronique Schiltz. Découvertes Gallimard Archéologie.

Or about the timeless myths of gods and goddesses

Dictionary of Classical Mythology, Pierre Grimal. Translated by A.R. Maxwell-Hyslop. Blackwell's.

A Voyage into the Past
of the Ukrainian Steppes

In the Stone Age

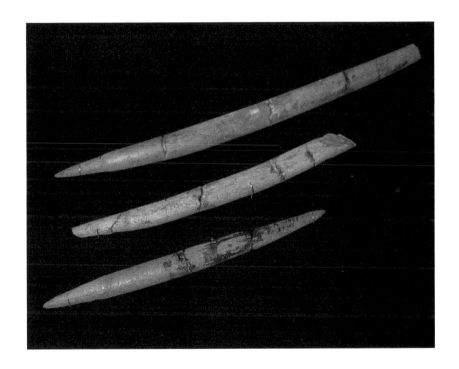

Hunting. Celebrating.

Some 20,000 years ago, the glaciers crept as far south as the Ukrainian steppes. Men banded together to track mammoths and bison, driving the animals into a ravine, for instance, where they could finish them off with their spears. Mammoths were prized for both their meat and their huge bones. They could be used to build homes, but also, it would appear, to make musical instruments!

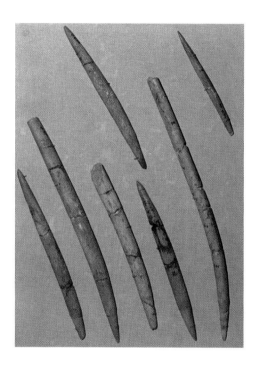

....

Spearheads

These spearheads were found along with masses of bison bone fragments. Many were sharpened on one side and some had tiny stones called microliths *attached to the surface with resin.*

Amvrossievka camp, Donetsk province (1940, 1948-1949)
21,000 - 20,000 B.C.
Bone, horn
Length 130-310 mm; width 10-20 mm
IA NUAS, Inv. No. AM-62/508-513; No.2326/6540

N.B. The abbreviation IA NUAS refers to the collection of the Institute of Archaeology, National Ukrainian Academy of Sciences.

Previous page
Spearheads, detail

Was the Original Xylophone a "Mammothophone"?

Some 20,000 years ago, these bones belonged to a young mammoth. Various clues lead archaeologists to believe that they are from one of the oldest sets of percussion instruments in the world.

These primitive percussion instruments were found with the nearby "rattle bracelet" in the same dwelling. Could they be material evidence of one of humanity's first… jam sessions?

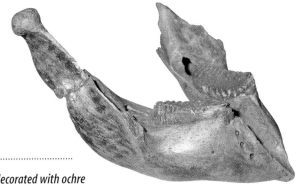

....

Mammoth bones, decorated with ochre

Dwelling No. 1, Mezine camp, Chernigov province (1954)
20,000 – 17,000 B.C.

The **mandible** would have been laid on its undecorated side and then struck on the top.

Dim. 500 x 300 mm
IA NUAS, Inv. No. AM-71/553

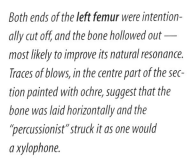

Both ends of the **left femur** were intentionally cut off, and the bone hollowed out — most likely to improve its natural resonance. Traces of blows, in the centre part of the section painted with ochre, suggest that the bone was laid horizontally and the "percussionist" struck it as one would a xylophone.

Dim. 800 x 200 mm
IA NUAS, Inv. No. AM-72/554

The **left shoulder blade** seems to have been held vertically, by the neck, much as one would hold a bass fiddle. In this case, too, traces of blows suggest that it was used as a percussion instrument.

Dim. 630 x 570 mm
IA NUAS, Inv. No. AM-75A/559

From Mammoth Tusk…

Along with the mammoth-bone "instruments," archaeologists discovered fragments that they painstakingly reassembled into a bracelet, which its wearer may once have shaken to keep the beat. The physical traces also allowed them to reconstruct the way such noise-makers might have been made.

....

Section of a mammoth tusk, engraved with geometric designs

The different "blocks" of motifs all along this section may have been intended for use in making a number of bracelets.

Dwelling No.1, Mezine camp, Chernigov province (before 1973)
15,000 B.C.
Dim. 120 x 50 x 48 mm
IA NUAS, Inv. No. AM-51/432

A mammoth tusk, like any tooth, consists of superposed layers of ivory. The artist seems to have made use of this structure by carving designs into the surface of the tusk and then removing a thin layer of decorated ivory. Holes were made in the ends of the fragments, which were then put together to make a bracelet that rattled when shaken. Then the process started over again: carve a new layer on the tusk, separate the fragment from the tusk and so on.

Separate bits of ivory were found bearing a design resembling needles on a fir tree branch. The same pattern can be seen on the pieces of the reassembled bracelet.

… to a "Rattle Bracelet"

....

Mammoth ivory bracelet

Dwelling No.1, Mezine camp, Chernigov province (before 1973)
15,000 B.C.
Dim. 83 x 33 mm
IA NUAS, Inv. No. AM-52/433

In the Time
of the Tripolye People

9,000 B.C.   2,500 B.C.

Sowing. Putting Down Roots.

About 9,000 B.C., a quiet revolution occurred in the Near East and in different places around the globe, as humans realized that they could sow their own crops instead of roaming in search of food. Humans became cultivators, and put down roots themselves.

Sometime around the 4th millennium B.C., the Neolithic revolution reached the forest steppes of Ukraine. People who had learned to farm and to make terra-cotta objects began building dwellings on the slopes above river valleys. Here they could grow their crops in the fertile loess, with ready access to water and a clear view of anyone approaching. This was the beginning of the Tripolye civilization, named after a village near Kiev where traces of it were first discovered. Skilled Tripolye hands shaped clay treasures in a style that, while reminiscent of artifacts from the Balkans, was nevertheless distinctive enough to lead archaeologists to consider this the great Neolithic civilization of Ukraine.

Figurines

With their wide hips, rounded buttocks and marked sexual organs, these two Venus figures are quite likely associated with some great fertility goddess. Their heads and features are stylized: a pinch for a nose, cuts to mark the eyes and mouth. The ample figurines recline on "chairs," one of which is topped with bull horns. Its occupant is holding something in her hands.

Left: figurine: length 95 mm; seat: length 70 mm, width 50 mm
IA NUAS, Inv. No. AM 196/1048; AM 196/1049

Right: figurine: length 80 mm; seat: length 50 mm, width 35 mm
IA NUAS, Inv. No. AM 195/1044; AM 195/1047

Village of Sabatinovka II, Odessa province (1948)
4,000 – 3,750 B.C.
Clay

Previous page
Female Tripolye figure

From Stone to Clay

Plentiful and easily worked, clay was the preferred material of Tripolye people, who turned it into dishes and figurines and used it to make their own homes.

....

Stone vessel

Pre-dating the Tripolye culture, this deep and pointed vessel was probably used in preparing food.

Soura Island, Dniepropetrovsk province (1958-1959)
5,500 – 5,000 B.C.
Stone
Height 180 mm; diam. 130 mm
IA NUAS, Inv. No. AM-127/858

....

Cover

This cover was made from carefully kneaded clay, with a bit of fine sand added to the mixture. This technique is characteristic of ceremonial dishes. A similar cover is presented in the exhibition.

Cover exhibited
Village of Bernachevka, Vinnitsa province (1989-1990)
3,000 – 2,900 B.C.
Clay
Height 58 mm; diam. 190 mm
IA NUAS, Inv. No. AM 2249/6395

....

Double vessel

Containers connected in the middle, such as these, have been found in various Neolithic cultures, although their purpose is still unknown. No one could drink from them, needless to say. Many archaeologists believe that they were used for ritual purposes, for spreading liquids or aromatics during fertility rites, for instance. The vessel exhibited is very similar to this one.

Vessel exhibited
Village of Vessely Kout,
Cherkassy province (1977)
3,250 – 2,900 B.C.
Clay
Height 270 mm;
length 280 mm;
width 120 mm
IA NUAS, Inv. No. AM 2033/4533

Decorated Vessel

Three years after archaeologists unearthed a lid, another site yielded up a surprise: a vessel that turned out to be a perfect match! Together, the two may represent a goddess. Between her "breasts," pointing in all four directions, the oval may represent the masculine dimension.

Cover
Village of Chkarovka,
Kiev province (1971)
3,250 – 3,000 B.C.
Clay
Height 90 mm; diam. 145 mm
IA NUAS, Inv. No. AM 2225/6367

Vessel
Village of Vessely Kout,
Cherkassy province (1974)
3,250 – 3,000 B.C.
Clay
Height 220 mm; diam. 250 mm
IA NUAS, Inv. No. AM 2024/6366

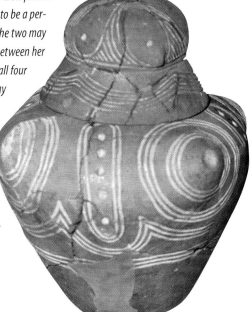

Lovely Human-Shaped Figurines

Delightful anthropomorphic figurines have been unearthed at Tripolye archaeological sites. Some of them have holes in them at the shoulders and hips, indicating that they may have been amulets, worn on a cord to ward off ill fortune.

Female figurine

The artist added quartz to the clay to make this white female figurine. Note the characteristic pinched nose, added-on breasts and shapely hips.

Village of Troyanov, Zhitomir province (1957)
3,000 - 2,600 B.C.
Clay
Height 185 mm
IA NUAS, Inv. No. AM 307/1304

Anthropomorphic figurine

Village of Bernachevka, Vinnitsa province (1993)
3,000 – 2,600 B.C.
Clay
Height 153 mm
IA NUAS, no Inv. No.

IA NUAS

Fragment of a figurine showing a nursing mother

Village of Bondarka, Cherkassy province (1984)
3,000 – 2,600 B.C.
Clay
Height 50 mm
IA NUAS, no Inv. No.

IA NUAS

... Including These Rare "Portraits"

Only about forty such figurines have been found, representing a later stage in the Tripolye culture. With their low brows, jutting chins and sharp noses, is this what the people looked like in the village of Maydanetz, where these pieces were discovered?

....

Fragments of anthropomorphic figurines

Village of Maydanetz, Cherkassy province (1986, 1987)
3,000 - 2,800 B.C.
Clay mixed with fine sand

Here we see a woman with a Tripolye hairstyle: parted down the middle, her long tresses (she was dark-haired, as far as can be told from the remaining traces of the slip) were tied quite low, near her waist. One of the legs of this statuette, found in the same place, measured 135 mm, suggesting that the entire piece was 350 to 400 mm tall. Seeds were mixed with the clay, as can be seen where one breast is missing.

Height 100 mm
IA NUAS, Inv.
No. II/12

A twisted nose and very rough features... here the artist was less painstaking.

Height 80 mm
IA NUAS, Inv. No. II/11

Given the lack of a woman's hairstyle, this must be a man's face. Once again, the original reddish-brown slip has almost completely disappeared. Similar figures have been found at Tripolye sites in Moldavia.

Height 40 mm
IA NUAS, Inv. No. II/34

Animal Shapes

Pieces left behind by Tripolye artists also include animal-shaped figurines, indicating that people of the time were gradually becoming herders as well as farmers. Over time, fewer and fewer bones from wild game turn up in the "kitchen garbage" at Neolithic sites, and more and more bones from domesticated animals. Humans were gradually learning to capture the wild ancestors of sheep, goats and cows.

....

Figurines of cows and calves

Simple but effective modelling reveals the age and sex of these cattle. Very similar figurines, discovered in Vinnitsa and Cherkassy provinces and dating from 3,100 to 2,800 B.C., each about 40 mm high, are presented in the exhibition.

Collection of the IA NUAS

....

Ewe's head

This wonderfully realistic head was probably attached to a vessel or part of a figurine. Its high-quality clay was covered with a brown slip. The design at the base of the neck doubtless represents the rope used to tie up the animal.

Village of Maydanetz, Cherkassy province (1984)
3,100 - 2,850 B.C.
Clay
Height 40 mm
IA NUAS, Inv. No. AM 2255/6401

....

Zoomorphic vessel

The lines may represent the animal's ribs, or perhaps ropes securing its load. Then again, they may have simply been the artist's fancy.

Village of Krinitchki, Odessa province (1909-1913)
3,250 - 2,800 B.C.
Clay
Height 55 mm; length 125 mm; width 75 mm
IA NUAS, Inv. No. AM 234/1136

In the Bronze Age

Transforming Matter. Moving with the Herds.

The next phase in the history of the Ukrainian steppes began in the second millennium B.C., as Tripolye villages broke up under growing pressure from tribes of semi-nomadic herders.

The social structure of these herders was quite different from that of the Tripolye people. For these newcomers, agriculture was simply a way of supplementing their diet, and they were not always welcome neighbours. To feed their large herds they had to be constantly on the move, in search of new pastures… even if the pasture was already taken! This led to a more military form of social organization on the steppes, with tribes led by chieftains. The transformation came at much the same time as the discovery of an alloy that could be used to produce more powerful tools—including tools for killing. Bronze.

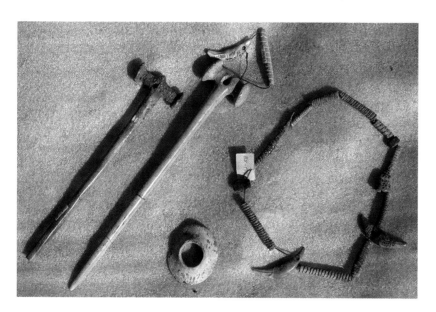

Previous page
Bronze spearhead

Collection of the IA NUAS

Jewellery

Needles, a necklace, part of a belt… Nothing in these simple ornaments suggests the splendour of the jewels that would be discovered in later kurgans. But this is how people adorned themselves several thousand years ago.

Kurgan No. 5, village of Mayorovka, Nikolayev province (1980)
23rd - 16th century B.C.
Bone, horn, teeth
Needles : length 200 mm, 160 mm; diam. 8 mm; IA NUAS, Inv. No. 665/46, 556-A
Necklace : 12 x length 20-40 mm, diam. 55 mm; 3 x length 30-35 mm; 3 x length 12 mm, diam. 10 mm; IA NUAS, Inv. No. 665/46, 556-A
Belt fragment : 44 x 38 mm; diam. opening 16 mm; IA NUAS, Inv. No. 665/12

Who Was He?

This human skull covered in clay is a remnant of a funeral rite practised by members of what was known as the Ingulye Catacomb Grave Culture, dating from the last quarter of the 3rd millennium and the first half of the 2nd millennium B.C. The models for this rite, with its impressive results, were most often religious figures or leaders.

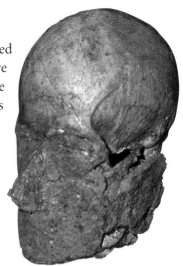

....

Arrow-making set

Among the kurgans from the Ingulye Catacomb Grave Culture are the tombs of craftspeople who had mastered the art of working flint, to produce extremely sharp arrow-heads. Once an arrowhead was finished, it was attached with string and resin to a shaft decorated with ochre.

Such sets of arrow-making tools, with the raw materials, tools and arrowheads at various stages of completion, have often been found in bags. But as flint was gradually aban-doned for bronze, the tombs of these "arrow-masters" also became much less common.

Large kurgan, village of Vladimirovka, Zaporozhye province (1981)
20th - 18th century B.C.
Flint, limestone, schist, bone, wood, bronze
IA NUAS, Inv. No. 41, 44/1-13, 45, 46, 47, 51, 52, 54, 55, 58, 59, 60

....

Human skull with clay mask

The head was detached from the body and the scalp removed. All the soft external and internal tissues (muscles, brain) were cleaned away from the skull. Then a paste of clay mixed with ochre or charcoal was smeared over the bones, to sculpt the forehead, nose, cheeks, the eyes (open or closed), the mouth and so on. Finally, the face was painted, most often in red, and the scalp was re-attached to the top of the skull. Archaeologists believe that this form of "sculpture" was intended to preserve the individual's features for posterity and at the same time mark his separation from the land of the living.

Kurgan, village of Zhovtiyevoye, Zaporozhye province (1981)
20th - 18th century B.C.
Height 225 mm
IA NUAS, Inv. No. AM 1972/4452

....

Stone hammer

This hammer was polished with care. A very similar hammer is exhibited.

Hammer exhibited
Kurgan, village of Novogrigorievka, Nikolayev province (1981)
Ingulye Catacomb Grave Culture
Dim. 95 x 45 mm; diam. opening 22 mm
IA NUAS, Inv. No. AM 1981/4466 (No.52)

Enduring Motifs

Decorated vessel

The swastika *on this vessel is a motif that has been used since antiquity—in Mesopotamia and Egypt for instance, and especially in India. (The word in fact comes from Sanskrit.) This is not surprising, for it is simple to draw and convincingly conveys a sense of motion. Today, the swastika is inevitably a sad reminder of the Nazis, but Hitler actually turned its arms in the other direction.*

Kurgan, village of Vilna Ukrayna, Kherson province (1971)
15th - 14th century B.C.
Ceramic
Height 175 mm; diam. 195 mm
IA NUAS, Inv. No. 662

Burner for aromatics *(above)*
The main section would be filled with fuel, and the small cavity, with the aromatics.

Kurgan, town of Lugansk, Lugansk province (1971)
Donetsk Catacomb Grave Culture
20th - 18th century B.C.
Ceramic, ochre
Height 71 mm; diam. 200 mm
IA NUAS, Inv. No. Mikol-71 No.50

Vessel with geometric design *(below)*

Kurgan No. 3, village of Akhtovo, Nikolayev province (1987)
20th - 18th century B.C.
Ceramic, ochre
Height 180 mm; diam. 115 mm
IA NUAS, no Inv. No.

Mould for "noise-making pendant"

Settlement of Verkhnetarassovka, Dniepropetrovsk province (1969)
14th - 12th century B.C.
Talc schist
Dim.125 x 72 mm
IA NUAS, Inv. No. 3/1

Occupation: Bronze Smith

Dating back to the Neolithic period, copper was the first metal used to make weapons, tools and ornaments. It was a logical choice: copper is one of the few metals that can be found naturally in its pure state—for instance, on the island of Cyprus, whose Latin name, cuprum, is actually the root of the word *copper*. And since it has a low melting point, it requires little fuel.

Smelting bronze, on the other hand, is a more demanding task. The smith must mix four parts copper with one part tin and work at higher temperatures. But the end result is an **alloy** with greater strength. And, just as important, the necessary material—clay for the oven and soft stone moulds—can be transported on foot. This advantage helped to make bronze the preferred material on the steppes until late antiquity, well after the advent of iron, which is much more difficult to make and demands much more fuel.

....

Mould for dagger

Village of Zagradovka, Kherson province; chance find (1970)
14th - 12th century B.C.
Talc schist
Dim. 255 x 58 mm
IA NUAS, Inv. No. IE

IA NUAS

....

Bronze blade

Kurgan, village of Velikaya Belozerka, Zaporozhye province (1972)
15th - 14th century B.C.
Dim. 158 x 35 mm
IA NUAS, Inv. No. 915/159

In the Time
of the Cimmerians

9th century B.C.

7th century B.C.

United Forever: the Warrior and His Horse

The archaeological sites attributed to the Cimmerian culture are essentially warriors' tombs containing bronze artifacts and the skeletons of lavishly decorated horses. For in life as in death, the Cimmerians adorned their mounts as richly as themselves. Take these bracelets and harnesses with matching geometric motifs—among the most beautiful examples of this non-figurative art.

....

Sword blade and bracelets
The hilt of this sword has disappeared, but the two-edged blade remains.

Two-edged sword blade
Village of Medvine, Kiev province; chance find (1985)
9th – early 8th century B.C.
Bronze
Dim. 390 x 36 mm
IA NUAS, Inv. No. 1082

Bracelets
Settlement of Soubbotov, Cherkassy province (1971)
9th century B.C.
Bronze
Dim. 92 x 69 mm; 74 x 52 mm
IA NUAS, Inv. No. TV-1677

Previous page
Harness trapping

Decorated whip handle

The whip was a nomad's companion. The fearsome nagayka
*was long used by warriors on the steppes to decapitate
their enemies.*

Kurgan No. 1, village of Zolnoye, near Simferopol, Crimea (1959)
Second half of 8th century - early 7th century B.C.
Bone
Diam. ring 35 mm
IA NUAS, Inv. No. 445/18/19/20/25/30

Harness trappings; detail

*Very early on, the nomads harnessed their steeds, to better
control them.*

Kurgan No. 1, village of Zolnoye, near Simferopol, Crimea (1959)
Second half of 8th century - early 7th century B.C.
Bone, ochre
Dim. lozenge-shaped plaques, 90 x 67 mm, 90 x 70 mm, 89 x 75 mm
Dim. C-shaped plaques, 60 x 25 mm, 55 x 25 mm, 57 x 23 mm
IA NUAS, Inv. No. 445/11, 5, 10; 445/21, 23, 24

Why Does This Pot-Bellied Container Have Four Necks?

A logical question. Unfortunately, no one really knows yet.

....

Vessel with several openings
This vessel may have been intended for ritual uses.
The interior is undivided.

Kurgan No. 1, settlement of Velikaya Alexandrovka, Kherson province (1981)
8th century B.C.
Ceramic
Height 335 mm; diam. 390 mm
IA NUAS

....

Ritual axe
Unlike other Cimmerian pieces, this ritual axe bears
zoomorphic designs.

Village of Doudarkov, Kiev province; chance find (1961)
9th - 7th century B.C.
Stag horn
Dim. 145 x 60 mm
IA NUAS, Inv. No. 35

In the Time
of the Scythians

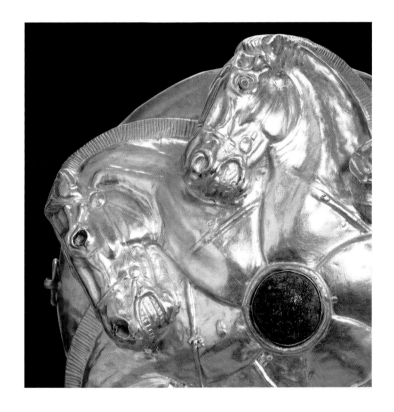

Discovering the Treasures of the Scythians

Like the Cimmerians before them and other nomads after them, Scythian riders roamed the steppes with their women, children, belongings and herds, moving at the languid pace of their wagons or charging at a furious gallop…
The grasses and the snow have retained no trace of the constant comings and goings of the tribes. Only the mounds of earth hold clues to the lives of the Scythian chieftains. Beneath these circular kurgans are tombs, sometimes containing sumptuous treasures, riches that would be discovered more than 2,000 years after Herodotus witnessed and carefully recorded their terrible burial rites.

The stag, like the nomads themselves, ventured out of the forest in search of pastures and water. Perhaps it was because of this bond that stags are a constant feature in the art of the steppes, all the way to China. In fact, stones bearing the stylized image of animals with antlers were erected on the central Asian steppes long before the Scythians occupied the plains north of the Black Sea. They were particularly common in Mongolia, where they were used to mark gravesites.

The stance of this bronze stag, a detail from the two finials on the next page, with its legs drawn up as if in full gallop and its glorious antlers spread out behind, is characteristic of the stag-like shapes often seen in Scythian animal art. Other examples are displayed in the exhibition. The nomads no doubt felt some connection with the image of freedom and speed…

Previous page
Phiale with six horse heads; detail

Evidence of Sumptuous Rituals and Burials

Below (piece not shown in the exhibition) This well-known Scythian finial shows the god Papaios in its centre. He was the King of the Scythian gods, the counterpart of Zeus in Greek mythology.

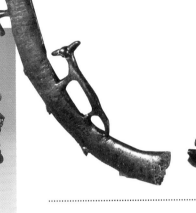

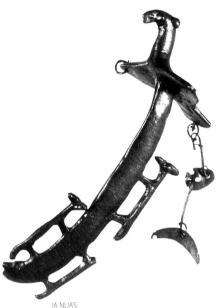

IA NUAS

V. Terebenine/History Museum, Kiev

Branches of a finial

This finial, adorned with wolves and birds in a symbolic representation of the "Tree of the World," doubtless graced the pole used by some shaman, with every piece jingling throughout the ritual. Although only these two branches were found, we can assume that the piece was likely as loaded down as the one shown on this page.

Village of Marianskoye, Dniepropetrovsk province; chance find (1963)
4th century B.C.
Bronze
Length 200 mm, 230 mm
IA NUAS, Inv. No. AM 774/6528-6530

Finials

These open-work finials decorated two corners of a funeral cart. Such pieces are often found in pairs or in sets of four.

Berdiansk kurgan, town of Berdiansk, Zaporozhye province (1977-1978)
First quarter of 4th century B.C.
Bronze
Height 189 mm
IA NUAS, Inv. No. 1159/63-64

Sacrificial meals

In his *Histories,* Herodotus tells how all the peoples of Scythia sacrificed cattle and other animals, including horses, by strangling the beast, butchering it and cooking the flesh in cauldrons. Since wood was very hard to come by on the steppes, bones were sometimes used as fuel. And if no cauldron was available, the victim itself was used: the flesh was all put into the animal's paunch, mixed with water and cooked.

Purification by hashish

According to Herodotus, the Scythians purified themselves following a burial by breathing smoke from hemp seeds sprinkled on burning stones, in a tent. The Greek states that the nomads would howl with joy in what looked to him like a steam bath, and which was doubtless a shamanic ritual. Archaeologists have found the stakes and felt walls from such tents, and cauldrons full of stones and seeds.

Ritual platter and knives

Repiakhovataya Mogila site, village of Matoussov, Cherkassy province (1974)
7th – early 6th century B.C.

Platter
Dim. 340 x 244 mm; stone; IA NUAS, Inv. No. 857/41

Knives
Length 360 mm, 410 mm; bronze; IA NUAS, Inv. No. 857/79-80

Vorvarka

It is not known for sure what such pierced cones were used for. They may have had some religious significance.

Kurgan No. 3, village of Chelugui, Zaporozhye province (1987)
4th century B.C.
Gold
Height 65-58 mm, diam. 76-120 mm; weight 140.7 g
IA NUAS, Inv. No. KP-IV-382

Cauldron and ladle

One or more cauldrons were commonly placed in tombs. Note the two pairs of handles here, making it easier to carry and use. The ladle is topped with the graceful profile of a swan.

Cauldron
Kurgan No. 1, town of Kamenka on the Dniepr, Zaporozhye province (1986)
4th century B.C.
Bronze
Height 175 mm; diam. 120 mm
IA NUAS, Inv. No. ZPE-86, c. 1, p.6

Ladle
Kurgan No. 7, village of Kamennaya Balka, Nikolayev province (1976)
4th century B.C.
Bronze
Length 387 mm; diam. 54 mm
IA NUAS, Inv. No. 67

Horse and Rider

His horse was the nomad's most precious possession, a companion in peace and in battle. Man and beast were buried together beneath the steppes, adorned in their finest raiment, for the ultimate ride.

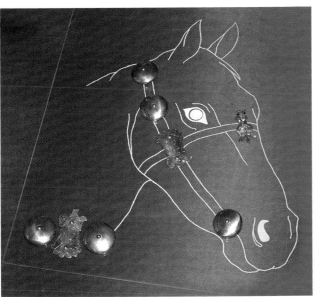

....

Reconstructed headgear for a horse; detail

At the base of the frontlet in the shape of a griffin (detail) is a hole for the strap. The cheekpieces are decorated with plant and bird motifs. Other harness trappings, found in Dniepropetrovsk province and conserved at the Institute, show evidence of deliberate blows on the back—traces of a ritual intended to "kill" the object when it was buried with the nomad and his horses.

Oguz kurgan, village of Nizhnie Serogozy, Kherson province (1980 – 1981)
Late third quarter of 4th century B.C.
Gold
Dim. and weight: griffin head, 65 x 33 x 38 mm, 73.94 g; cheekpiece, 84 x 55 mm, 84 x 56 mm, 87.82 g; round plaques, diam. 53 mm, 57 mm, 58 mm, 221.28 g
IA NUAS, Inv. No. Z-1161-1168

....

Horse frontlet

Herodotus tell us that the only gods worshipped by the Scythians were Hestia, Zeus, Earth (wife of Zeus), Apollo, Celestial Aphrodite, Heracles and Ares. The Royal Scythians also worshipped Poseidon, or "Thagimasadas," in their language. This fish-shaped frontlet from a horse's harness may be a reference to the god of the sea whom Herodotus mentions, the incarnation of the "horse of the sea." Similar pieces have been found in other Royal Scythian kurgans.

Taranova Mogila site, village of Ingoulo-Kamenka, Kirovograd province (1989)
4th century B.C.
Gold
Dim. 340 x 17-58 mm; weight 34.67 g
IA NUAS, Inv. No. Z-15

Harness ornaments

The face on these pieces is Heracles. On the piece showing a younger-looking Heracles, holes were roughly pierced, most likely because the rear attachment was missing. A similar, but intact, plaque is also exhibited.

Babina Mogila site, village of Tarasso-Grigorievka, Dniepropetrovsk province (1986)
4th century B.C.
Silver, gold
Diam. 75 mm; weight 34.68 g, 64.40 g
IA NUAS, Inv. No. KP-IV-384, 385

The feats of Heracles

Heracles, or Hercules, as the Romans knew him, is certainly the most famous hero of Greek mythology. Legend has it that as an infant, he was suckling Hera one day while she was asleep. When she awoke, she pushed him away, and the trail of milk he left behind became the Milky Way up in the sky.

Among Heracles' many feats were his "twelve labours," beginning with his victory over a monstrous lion that was terrorizing the valley of Nemea. He squeezed the lion to death with his bare hands, and donned its skin and mane. Another of his labours, mentioned by Herodotus, is related to the origins of the Scythians. He had been driving an enormous herd back to Greece when he arrived in Scythia, where it was bitterly cold. He rolled himself up in his lion's skin and went to sleep. When he awoke, he found that his horses, which he had unharnessed for the night, had mysteriously disappeared. They had been taken by a viper-maiden, who agreed to return them if Heracles would lay with her. Their union produced three sons: Agathyrsus, Gelonus, and Scythes. Only Scythes, the youngest, succeeded in a task that Heracles had set for them, and became the ruler of the land and father of the line of Scythian kings.

Harness trappings

The lion's paws around the face and holding the cape identify this figure as Heracles (inset).

Babina Mogila site, village of Tarasso-Grigorievka, Dniepropetrovsk province (1986)
4th century B.C.
Silver
Dim. lion's-head plaques (10): 16 x 14 mm; weight 14.79 g
Dim. Heracles plaques (7): 29 x 25 mm; weight 32.07 g
Dim. gorgon's-head plaques (11): 20 x 18 mm; weight 21,18 g
IA NUAS, Inv. No. KP-IV-383, 387, 388

Bow and Arrow

The Scythians were remarkable archers. Even when galloping at full speed, they could loose volley after volley—sometimes even turning around to shoot behind them after passing the enemy, in one last unexpected and fatal "parting shot"!

They kept their bows and arrows in a quiver with two compartments, called a *gorytus*, worn hanging from a belt down the left thigh. The quiver was made of wood and covered with leather; ceremonial models were covered with gold.

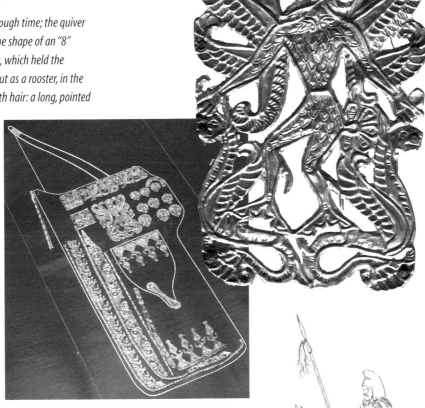

....

Decorations from a gorytus; detail

Only the gold has survived down through time; the quiver itself has disappeared. A plaque in the shape of an "8" marks the flap on the outside pocket, which held the arrows. Note the holy man, decked out as a rooster, in the centre (detail). His face is covered with hair: a long, pointed beard, a moustache, sideburns, with his tresses pulled back into a small knot at the base of his neck. His legs have been transformed into clawed feet, trampling two dragons.

Soboleva Mogila site, village of Gorniatskoye, Dniepropetrovsk province (1990-1991)
4th century B.C.
Gold
Weight 233.44 g
IA NUAS, Inv. No. Z-1968-1993, 1996

Beware of the parting shot!

Or is it a "Parthian shot"? The expression "parting shot," a surprise attack just when the victim assumes that the battle—verbal or otherwise—is over, may come from the Parthians, a people of Iranian origin who reached their peak in the 1st century B.C., and who warred with the Scythians. The image of a devastating blow delivered unexpectedly at the end of a discussion lives on in this popular expression.

Warriors, hunters and clever strategists

The Scythians were highly skilled strategists, judging by Herodotus' fascinating account of the campaign led against them by Darius I, King of the Persians from 521 to 486 B.C., as summarized below.

A huge Persian army marched on Scythia, determined to conquer the land and people. The Scythian kings, seeing the danger, sent their women, children and herds to safety in the north and dispatched their best warriors to remain a day's march ahead of the leading Persian soldiers, gradually withdrawing as the enemy advanced. Then began a real war of attrition. The heavy Persian army was unable to lay hold of the agile Scythian cavalry, who led the Persians farther on and then fled, harassing the opposing army day and night and laying waste to the land ahead of the invaders.

Clever strategists, the Scythians allowed the enemy to capture a few sheep from time to time, so as to give the starving Persians some sustenance as they were lured deeper into Scythian country. Finally, when the two camps stood face to face, the Scythian troops suddenly broke ranks and began chasing after a hare—one of their favourite pastimes! Throughout the campaign, playing on their speed and their unmatched knowledge of the steppes, they toyed with Darius. His rare "victories" were due to his donkeys, which terrified the horses with their unfamiliar braying sounds, and caused the Scythian mounts to rear up and bolt!

Darius, seeing no end to the aggravating tactics, sent a messenger to the Scythians. If the Scythians thought themselves strong enough to oppose him, he said, then let them fight! Otherwise, if they admitted that they were too weak, they should submit to their master. The Scythian kings flew into a rage at the mere mention of enslavement, said Herodotus. They sent a messenger back to Darius, bearing a bird, a mouse, a frog and five arrows. When asked what these "gifts" meant, the messenger replied that the Persians should simply use a bit of imagination. Darius thought that the Scythians were presenting him with earth (the mouse) and water (the frog), and intended to surrender—the rapid bird and the five arrows meaning that they were prepared to lay down their arms. But one of Darius' counsellors, Gobryas, disagreed, saying that the true meaning of the message was that unless the Persians could fly like birds, burrow into the ground like mice or hide in the water like frogs, they would be shot by Scythian arrows.

Gobryas was right. Darius started a long and difficult retreat back home.

....

Detail of a sword
The hilt of this sword in the Greek style is decorated with stags and a feline. The Scythians, reported Herodotus, worshipped Ares in the form of a sword driven into the top of an altar of brushwood. Each year they added fifty wagonloads of sticks, to maintain the altar at the same height.

Soboleva Mogila site, village of Gorniatskoye, Dniepropetrovsk province (1990-1991)
4th century B.C.
Iron, gold, silver
Length 667 mm; weight 26.66 g
IA NUAS, Inv. No. Z-1998, 1999

Mortal Combat

Scythian artists commonly depicted scenes in which a stag or horse was attacked by a lion, panther or winged griffin.

Decorated goblet

Aside from its obvious abundance of detail, this goblet bears a thoroughly geometric design, with four rows of creatures all under attack by lions: a bull, horse, deer and stag. The bottom also shows an attack scene.

Bratolubovsky kurgan, village of Olguino, Kherson province (1990)
5th century B.C.
Gold
Height 180 mm, diam. 132-185 mm; weight 625.12 g
IA NUAS, Inv. No. KP-IV-425

Decorated vessel; detail

Soboleva Mogila site, village of Gorniatskoye, Dniepropetrovsk province (1991-1992)
4th century B.C.
Silver, gold
Height 112.5 mm; diam. 102 mm
IA NUAS, Inv. No. KP-V-661A

Round-Bottomed Dishes

Kurgans have also yielded a wide variety of drinking vessels. For use by royalty or commoners, these vessels were often in rounded shapes: phiales and rhytons were designed to be held in the hand, set on a felt ring or hung up, where they would be protected from the swaying motion of the owner's horse or wagon.

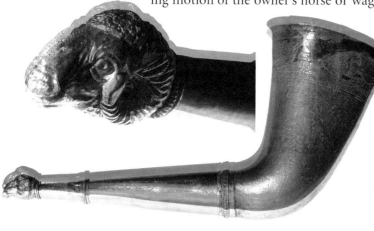

Rhyton

The tip of this rhyton is adorned with a beautiful ram's head. On the open end are scenes depicting animals fighting.

Soboleva Mogila site, village of Gorniatskoye, Dniepropetrovsk province (1991-1992)
4th century B.C.
Silver, gold
Dim. 190 x 115 mm
IA NUAS, Inv. No. KP-V-660

Reconstructed rhyton

The original piece was made of gold and silver. The plaques show a stag in its typical stance.

Bratolubovsky kurgan, village of Olguino, Kherson province (1990)
5th century B.C.
Gold, ceramic
Dim. 285 x 90 mm; weight gold, 21.61 g
IA NUAS, Inv. No. KP-IV-427

Draining the rhyton

The Scythians were fond of drink, particularly Greek wine. But Herodotus tells us that, unlike the Greeks, the nomads drank the thick wine "straight," instead of diluting it with water! Wine is still served in such horn-shaped containers in the Caucasus. But be careful—you're expected to empty it once you start drinking!

... Sometimes with Swirling Designs

Scythian art, with its curved and flowing lines, reflects the freedom of the nomads. A motif may even be repeated three, four or six times, in an endless cycle. For example, this master-piece immortalizes, like a series of snapshots, the vibrant spirit of the favourite companion of warriors and kings.

Phiale *bearing six horses' heads* (underside).
Such cups with rounded bottoms, used for ritual purposes,
also existed in more modest forms, for day-to-day use.

Bratolubovsky kurgan, village of Olguino, Kherson province (1990)
5th century B.C.
Gold, red amber
Height 48 mm, diam. 125 mm; weight 223 g
IA NUAS, Inv. No. KP-IV-426

Be-jewelled for the Voyage to the Hereafter

In many kurgans, archaeologists have found skeletons of women wearing rings, bracelets, earrings and other jewellery. Men and children have also been found, adorned with simple or sumptuous jewellery portraying creatures of the steppes or of the artist's imagination.

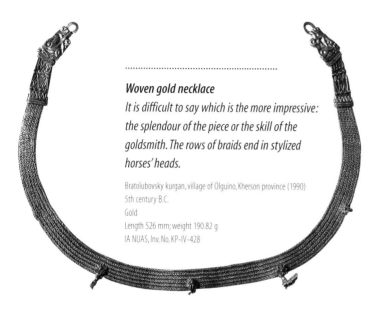

....

Woven gold necklace

It is difficult to say which is the more impressive: the splendour of the piece or the skill of the goldsmith. The rows of braids end in stylized horses' heads.

Bratolubovsky kurgan, village of Olguino, Kherson province (1990)
5th century B.C.
Gold
Length 526 mm; weight 190.82 g
IA NUAS, Inv. No. KP-IV-428

....

Child's spiral bracelets and necklace

Wolves recline at the tips of the bracelets, with their muzzles resting on their paws. The animal heads on the necklace are too stylized to be identified.

Soboleva Mogila site, village of Gorniatskoye, Dniepropetrovsk province (1990-1991)
4th century B.C.
Gold

Bracelets
Dim. 65 x 69 mm, 58 x 62 mm; weight 361.79 g; IA NUAS, Inv. No. Z-1829, 1830

Child's necklace
Dim. 80 x 86 mm; weight 47.57 g; IA NUAS, Inv. No. Z-2121

....

Torque and bracelet

One end of this tubular necklace or torque slides into the other up to a depth of four centimetres. Simple or sumptuous, such torques were worn mostly by men. The ends of this bracelet are open, so it is also simple to adjust.

Kurgan No. 10, village of Malaya Lepetikha, Kherson province (1992)
4th century B.C.
Gold

Torque
Diam. 105 mm; weight 277.05 g
IA NUAS Inv. No. KP-703/962

Bracelet
Diam. 60 mm; width 20 mm
weight 22.39 g;
IA NUAS, Inv. No. KP-703/3

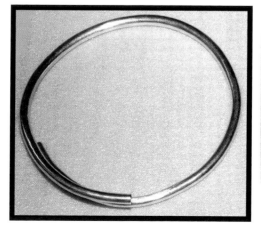

The Greek influence is obvious in these treasures, and with good reason: most of the finely worked gold objects discovered in Scythian kurgans were made by Greek goldsmiths, who adapted their skills to the tastes of their wealthy nomad customers. The result was original productions of the highest quality. Many motifs also show the attraction of the East: griffins, lotus flowers, bodies covered with feathers, fur or scales…

....

Child's necklace

The strikingly realistic shells are hollow, made of two halves joined together.

Oguz kurgan, village of Nizhnie Serogozy, Kherson province (1980-1981)
Late third quarter of 4th century B.C.
Gold
Dim. shells (9): 12 x 8 mm; weight 5.18 g
IA NUAS, Inv. No. Z-880-888

Gold, Beautiful and Everlasting

Cast, beaten, engraved or struck in identical patterns, solid gold or gold leaf applied to leather, wood or silver… seductive and eternally youthful, gold abounds in Scythian treasures. The kurgans have been so heavily looted, though, that only a tiny percentage of their treasures are housed in museums. We will never know how many priceless objects were stolen and hurriedly melted down.

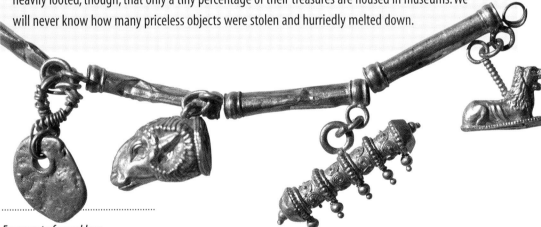

....

Fragment of a necklace

This fragment comes from a type of large necklace, holding pendants that doubled as amulets, that the Romans called crepundi. A flat disk, a ram's head, a tube with rings and a lion all hang from sheets of gold rolled and strung together like beads.

Oguz kurgan, village of Nizhnye Seogozy, Kherson province (1980-1981)
Late third quarter of 4th century B.C.
Gold
Length 21-21.5 mm; weight 14.93 g
IA NUAS, Inv. No. Z-1010-1013

Conical, Round, Cylindrical...

... women's head-dresses of all shapes have been found in kurgans, probably associated with noblewomen or high-ranking priestesses.

Reconstructed woman's head-dress, or calathos
The open-work bands featuring plant motifs are set off by 31 plaques with feline heads and 30 with human faces, a design repeated on the three half-spheres on top. The band along the lower edge also shows plant designs.

Tatianina Mogila site, town of Ordzhonikidze,
Dniepropetrovsk province (1986)
Mid-4th century B.C.
Gold
IA NUAS, Inv. No. Z-1669-1744

Diadem

This piece once adorned a woman's head-dress.

Babina Mogila site, village of Tarasso-Grigorievka, Dniepropetrovsk province (1986)
4th century B.C.
Gold
Dim. 195 x 29 mm; weight 56.38 g
IA NUAS, Inv. No. Z-1746

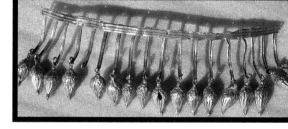

Plaque

This plaque, which adorned a woman's head-dress, may represent the goddess Cybele, "Mother of the Gods," goddess of abundance, personifying the power of all growing things. Plant motifs are transformed into stylized stags' heads with elaborate antlers.

Babina Mogila site, village of Tarasso-Grigorievka, Dniepropetrovsk province (1986)
4th century B.C.
Gold
Dim. 76 x 47-62 mm; weight 13.54 g
IA NUAS, Inv. No. Z-1745

Familiar Scenes

A galloping stag, a deer under attack, rosettes or lotus flowers with an oriental touch... Like jewellery, ornamental plaques are decorated with favourite scenes and motifs.

....

Plaques with pendants *(detail above, on right)*
On these plaques, each with four eyelets on the back,
a lion can be seen attacking a deer.

Kurgan No. 9, village of Malaya Lepetikha, Kherson province (1992)
4th century B.C.
Gold
Dim. 27 x 22 mm; weight 25.08 g
IA NUAS, Inv. No. KP-703/923, 925, 927, 928, 930

....

Belt plaque with stag design
The nomad's belt, of leather sometimes reinforced with
bronze or iron, had to be solidly fastened, for it held the
horseman's arms and various accoutrements at his waist.

Kurgan No. 9, village of Malaya Lepetikha, Kherson province (1992)
4th century B.C.
Gold
Dim. of plaques (2): 58 x 49 mm; weight 8.5 g
IA NUAS, Inv. No. KP-703/891-892

....

Open-work plaques
Four lotus flowers are arranged around the central
flower. What type and colour of fabric might
they originally have graced?

Oguz kurgan, village of Nizhnye Seogozy, Kherson province
(1980-1981)
Late third quarter of 4th century B.C.
Gold
Diam. 54 mm, 55 mm; weight 7.31 g
IA NUAS, Inv. No. Z-463-464

....

Rosette plaques

Oguz kurgan, village of Nizhnye Seogozy, Kherson province (1980-1981)
Late third quarter of 4th century B.C.
Gold
Dim. 21 x 15 mm, 18 x 15 mm; weight 5.18g
IA NUAS, Inv. No. Z-371-372

Intact among the Bones

Ornamental plaques are by far the most numerous objects found in kurgans—thousands of them scattered among the bones, although the threads that once attached them to cloth, felt or leather have long since rotted away.

....

Palmette plaques

Oguz kurgan, village of Nizhnye Seogozy, Kherson province (1980-1981)
Late third quarter of 4th century B.C.
Gold
Dim.of plaques (12): 19 x 12 mm; weight 5.69 g
IA NUAS, Inv. No. Z-1050-1061

....

Satyr's-head plaques; detail
An expressive representation of these lecherous characters from Greek mythology.

Oguz kurgan, village of Nizhnye Seogozy, Kherson province (1980-1981)
Late third quarter of 4th century B.C.
Gold
Dim. of plaques (10): 16-18 x 13-13.5 mm; weight 6.47 g
IA NUAS, Inv. No. Z-1037-1046

....

Lion's-head plaques; detail

Oguz kurgan, village of Nizhnye Seogozy, Kherson province (1980-1981)
Late third quarter of 4th century B.C.
Gold
Dim.of plaques (11): 19 x 18 mm; weight 6.09 g
IA NUAS, Inv. No. Z-1020-1030

The motifs were often obtained by stamping, i.e. by hammering sheets of gold on a die.

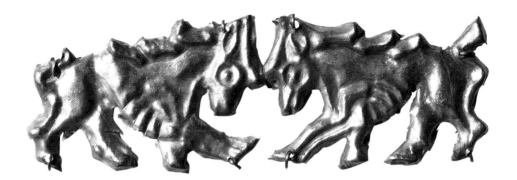

....

Plaques with playing kids

Eleven pairs of kids butt each other, each one's position slightly different from its opponent's. Steppes art often employed inverse symmetry for pairs of plaques meant for garments. These would have adorned a woman's head-dress.

Kurgan No. 1, village of Vladimirovka, Zaporozhye province (1980)
4th century B.C.
Gold
Dim. of plaques (22): 30 x 20 mm; weight 18.24 g
IA NUAS, Inv. No. Z-3187-3208

....

Plaques with a sphinx motif

These plaques adorned a Scythian woman's head-dress. The two sets differ in size and minute details.

Kurgan, village of Voltchansk, Zaporozhye province (1980)
4th century B.C.
Gold
Dim. 40-41 x 35-37 mm, 33-35 x 27-29 mm; weight 17.93 g
IA NUAS, Inv. No. Z-3444-3453

Dance of the Goddesses

Scythian men—fighting, hunting or milking—are regularly shown on objects found in tombs. Women, on the other hand, are almost completely absent from the art of the steppes. The king's companions may have been covered in gold when laid to rest with him in the kurgan, but it seems that only goddesses were honoured with a place on eternal gold.

Plaques in the shape of goddesses holding decorated poles or knives; detail

Kurgan No. 6, village of Vodoslavka, Kherson province (1983)
Late 5th - early 4th century B.C.
Gold
Dim. 46 x 30 mm, 42 x 25 mm; weight 10.34 g
IA NUAS, Inv. No. Z-2394-2398

Plaques showing dancing women; detail

These "possessed" women personified the orgiastic spirits of Nature, for the Greeks. Their stance and the drape of their fine tunics highlight their graceful forms and movements. Similar plaques are considered to have served as ornaments on a priestess' head-dress.

Oguz kurgan, village of Nizhnye Seogozy, Kherson province (1980-1981)
Late third quarter of 4th century B.C.
Gold
Dim. 34 x 16 mm, 49 x 20 mm, 33 x 15 mm; weight 3.09 g
IA NUAS, Inv. No. Z-365-367

A Walking Fortune

Nomads obviously couldn't lug around a safe!
Instead, they had to carry their riches and currency on themselves,
in the form of many small golden objects. Some were jewellery, of course,
but also *plaques* that were nearly as good as jewellery.

Reconstructed woman's head-dress or calathos
The rectangular plaques are decorated with stags.

Kurgan No. 1, town of Kamenka on the Dniepr, Zaporozhye province (1986);
plaques from head-dress trains: Tatianina Mogila site, Dnepropetrovsk province,
town of Ordzhonikidze (1968)
4th century B.C.
Gold
IA NUAS, Inv. No. Z-299-336, 337-354

Ring

*This smooth, round ring, easily adjustable, was the most
popular model among Scythians in the 4th century B.C.
Two other identical rings are exhibited.*

Kurgan No. 1, town of Kamenka on the Dniepr, Zaporozhye province (1986)
4th century B.C.
Gold
Diam. 17 mm; weight 2.98 g
IA NUAS, Inv. No. Z-356

Earrings

*Earrings of the time were frequently boat-shaped,
sometimes with pendants added. In this admirably elegant
crescent design, the hook on one end fits into the loop on
the other.*

Kurgan No. 1, town of Kamenka on the Dniepr, Zaporozhye province (1986)
4th century B.C.
Gold
Height 55 mm; weight 15.59 g
IA NUAS, Inv. No. Z-297, 298

Reconstructed shoes

Tatianina Mogila site, town of Ordzhonikidze, Dnepropetrovsk province (1986)
Mid-4th century B.C.
Gold
Dim. of plaques (22): 15 x 15 mm; weight 9.68 g
IA NUAS, Inv. No. Z-1181, 1183-1188, 1192, 1194-1196, 1198-1200, 1202-1203,
1205-1209, 1212

Headband

*Decorated with griffins and chimera and worn as
part of a head-dress.*

Dim. 300 x 39 mm; weight 19.93 g
Kurgan No. 1, town of Kamenka on the Dniepr, Zaporozhye province
(1986)
4th century B.C.
Gold
IA NUAS, Inv. No. Z-296

Treasures from the Ukrainian Steppes

On the Shores
of the Black Sea

7th century B.C.

Winds from the East, Winds from the West

Beginning in the 7th century B.C., long after they had established themselves in Asia Minor, the Greeks ventured across the dangerous fogs of the Black Sea— which they baptized Pontos Euxeinos, *the "hospitable sea," in hopes of taming it.*

They founded flourishing ports on its fertile shores and at the mouths of navigable routes leading northward into the forests.

Many digs have been conducted on the sites of these Greek colonies, including Olbia, where Herodotus stayed when he was studying the Scythians. Finds there have included marble and terracotta treasures, memories of gods, goddesses and legends…

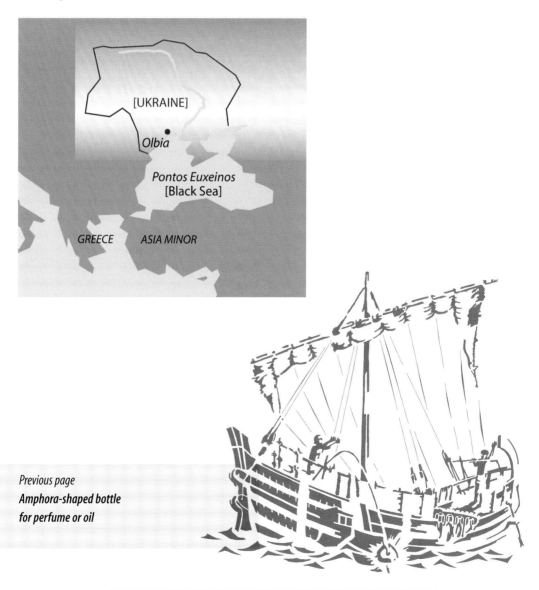

Previous page
**Amphora-shaped bottle
for perfume or oil**

Import-Export Trade

The port of Olbia quickly became an important crossroads between the nomads of the steppes and Mediterranean traders. Greek ships unloaded amphorae of olive oil and wine, the latter much appreciated by the nomads—in fact, the Greeks say of a hard drinker that he "drinks like a Scythian"! Then they left again, loaded down with timber, wheat and slaves. Caravans from the heart of Asia made their way to Olbia too, bringing furs and taking away ceramics, bronze mirrors and other goods.

....

Decorated chalice

... typical of the Greek island of Chios. In the early days of Greek colonization, most pieces were imported. The dancers are comastes.

Ancient Berezan Island site, Nikolayev province (1955)
6th century B.C.
Ceramic
Height 106 mm; diam. 110 mm
IA NUAS, Inv. No. AM-983/1288

....

Restored fragment of a dinos

A dinos was used to dilute wine, which was too thick and strong to be drunk straight. This one is typical of the goods produced in Clazomenae, in Asia Minor. Its friezes show lotus flowers, horsemen, women playing the zither, etc.

Ancient Berezan Island site, Nikolayev province (1970)
6th century B.C.
Ceramic
Height 260 mm; diam. 382 mm
IA NUAS, Inv. No. AB/70-480 (AM 1021/6156)

Under Aphrodite's Gaze

Life in the Greek colonies on the Black Sea was every bit as good as "back home" and in the outposts of Asia Minor. Architecture, theatre and music flourished, and Greek women made themselves more beautiful than ever! Just consider these objects, which would almost appear at home on any dressing table today.

....

Head of an Aphrodite, from Syria

Olbia site, village of Paroutino, Nikolayev province (1981)
4th - 3rd century B.C.
Terracotta
Height 65 mm
IA NUAS, Inv. No. O-95/r-25/1062

Mirror

When this mirror, discovered in a kurgan, was first delivered by the bronze smith, it must have glittered like gold! Mirrors were often left in women's graves. Their ability to reflect the owner's features probably gave them some magic power, which is why they are also associated with representations of priestesses.

Kurgan No. 4, village of Ivanovka (1983)
6th - 4th century B.C.
Bronze
Diam. 213 mm; length of handle 130 mm
IA NUAS, Inv. No. LPE-83

....

Hair pins

Olbia site, village of Paroutino, Nikolayev province (1994)
1st - 3rd century A.D.
Ivory
Length 75 mm, 100 mm
IA NUAS, Inv. No. AM-1065/5213; O-94/r-25/789

....

Decorated comb

Bearing designs of an open-winged duck and what looks like a mushroom on its other side, this comb was probably made in Parthia.

Olbia site, village of Paroutino, Nikolayev province (1965)
3rd century A.D.
Bone
Dim. 74 x 61 x 4 mm
IA NUAS, Inv. No. AM-1063/5211

According to Herodotus, Scythian women "washed" by plastering their bodies with a fragrant paste made of cypress, cedar and frankincense. When they removed it the next day, their skin was clean and glossy. The Greeks had other habits. After a real bath, Greek women liked to anoint themselves with perfumed oil, to protect themselves from the sun's drying rays. They wore make-up, too, colouring their cheeks and lips with rouge, darkening their eyebrows and whitening their faces to make themselves look paler.

Fibula

An unusual discovery in the ancient sites on the Black Sea, this clasp in the form of a peacock comes from one of the western provinces of the Roman Empire.

Necropolis, village of Zolotoye, Crimea (1970)
1st - 2nd century A.D.
Bronze
Dim. 30 x 5-19 mm
IA NUAS, Inv. No. Zol.-70-255

Bottles for perfume or oil

The one on the left is called an alabastron. *The one on the right is shaped like an amphora. They were discovered together. Bottles like these are often found in tombs.*

Olbia site, village of Paroutino, Nikolayev province (1992)
5th century B.C.
Glass paste
Height 110 mm, 102 mm
IA NUAS, Inv. No. O-92/Necr. 77, 79

Enamelled fibulae *(above and on left)*

These clasps were also produced in the western provinces of the Roman Empire. Enamelling first began during the Roman epoch.

Olbia site, village of Paroutino, Nikolayev province (1985)
1st - 2nd century A.D.
Bronze, enamel
Dim. 48 x 42-48 mm; 40 x 25 mm
IA NUAS, Inv. No. AM-1029/3905; O-85/Necr./179

Ornament *(below)*

Is this ornament part of a fibula? Did it adorn a garment? The face depicted evokes that of the sun god, Helios.

Olbia site, village of Paroutino, Nikolayev province (1993)
1st - 3rd century A.D.
Ivory
Dim. 23-25 x 20 x 2-5 mm
IA NUAS, Inv. No. O-93/r-25/759

Necklaces

Among women's favourite pieces of jewellery are necklaces. A greater variety of materials was used as time went on.

Necropolis, village of Zolotoye, Crimea (1970, 1971)
Various epochs: 2nd — 1st century B.C. – 1st century A.D.
Carnelian, rock crystal, amber, glass, glass paste, faience
IA NUAS, Inv. No. Zol.-70-143, 253, 47, Zol.-71-657, 675

Timeless Tales of Gods and Goddesses

Hermes, the trickster

Son of Zeus, King of the gods, and of Maia, youngest of the Pleiades, Hermes was an extraordinarily precocious child. On the very day he was born, he made his way to Thessaly, where his brother Apollo was watching his herds.

The shepherd was distracted by thoughts of love, and was not watching his flocks as closely as he should. Hermes made off with twelve cows, one hundred heifers and a bull. Driving his spoils through Greece, he sacrificed some of them, shared the others among the gods, and fled. But on the way home, he found a tortoise in his path and killed it; across its emptied carapace he stretched strings made of gut from the intestines of the cattle he had slaughtered. And thus Hermes invented the lyre. Then he crept quietly back into his crib…

Hermes appeased Apollo's anger by giving him the lyre. Some time later, he invented the flute, for which Apollo traded his shepherd's crook and lessons in divining. And in this way Hermes became the god of trade. With his winged sandals, he is also the messenger of the gods.

···

Head of Hermes
Statues of Hermes, the protector of travellers, were often put up at crossroads in the form of a column bearing a human bust (this face was part of one such representation) and male organs. He has aged since his youthful follies (see inset)!

Olbia site, village of Paroutino, Nikolayev province (1996)
2nd - 3rd century A.D.
Marble
Height 178 mm
IA NUAS, Inv. No. O-96/r-25/441

···

Fragment of an eagle figurine
The figurine was probably produced in Asia Minor. The eagle was traditionally shown head on, with its wings spread and its head turned to the left—which is why the right eye of this figurine has a pupil.

Olbia site, village of Paroutino, Nikolayev province (1991)
2nd - 3rd century A.D.
Marble
Height 135 mm
IA NUAS, Inv. No. O-91/r-25/832

Hermaphroditus, Son of Hermes and Aphrodite

Today, the term hermaphrodite means a person who has both masculine and feminine characteristics. But for the people of the ancient world, it evoked a story almost as beautiful as this marble torso.

The Hazards of Bathing

Upon turning 15, Hermaphroditus decided to strike out and see the world. One day, he arrived at a magnificent lake, inhabited by a nymph, Salmacis. Enraptured by the young man's beauty, she made advances to him… and was rejected. Vexed, Salmacis withdrew. Hermaphroditus immediately disrobed and threw himself into the crystalline water. But Salmacis had actually hidden herself so as to watch him. Seeing him at her mercy, she caught and held the youth, praying to the gods that they "might become one flesh." Her prayer was answered and the two were transformed into a new being, both male and female.

Hermaphroditus, for his part, demanded of the gods that anyone who bathed in the lake would lose his virility. Lake Salmacis was long reputed to have this effect.

....

Torso of a hermaphrodite

This carefully polished hermaphrodite, unparalleled in the Black Sea region, comes from the workshops of Alexandria, in Egypt. Metal traces on its back indicate that the statue must have been fixed to a wall or a support of some kind.

2nd century B.C.
Olbia site, village of Paroutino, Nikolayev province (1974)
Marble
Height 300 mm
IA NUAS, Inv. No. O-74/AGD/218

....

Top central portion of a low-relief tile, showing Mithra slaying a bull

Here we see Mithra as he is usually portrayed, with a Phrygian cap on his head, plunging a dagger into the throat of a bull, symbol of the forces of darkness. The god of light of the ancient Persians was honoured in both the Greek and Roman empires. In fact, the date of Christmas may have been fixed to coincide with his feast day, on December 25.

Olbia site, village of Paroutino,
Nikolayev province (1990)
Late 2nd century - early 3rd century A.D.
Marble
Dim. 81 x 74 x 14-19 mm
IA NUAS, Inv. No. O-90/r-25/482

Product of Olbia

Demeter and her daughter, Persephone, were so closely linked in their adventures that they were often called "the two Goddesses." Here they appear as superb busts (mere mortals would have been shown complete), characteristic of terracotta artwork from the Olbia region.

Demeter, Goddess of Wheat

Daughter of Kronos, Time, Demeter was worshipped in all parts of the Greek world where wheat grew.

....

Bust of Demeter *(below)*
Like the Greeks of the time, the goddess wears a chiton, a robe consisting of simple pieces of cloth attached at the shoulders. On her head she wears a calathos.

Olbia site, village of Paroutino, Nikolayev province (1959)
3rd century B.C.
Terracotta
Height 185 mm
IA NUAS, Inv. No. O-59/3481, 4305, 4870

....

Bust of Demeter *(above)*
This other bust was made in a two-sided mould, with the surplus clay removed with a knife. Certain details were then added. The neck of her chiton was decorated with mother-of-pearl. Coloured traces can still be seen on the surface, although much has been eroded by moisture. Her arms were extended out in front.

Olbia site, village of Paroutino, Nikolayev province (1993)
3rd century B.C.
Terracotta
Height 325 mm
IA NUAS, Inv. No. O-93/r-25/2918

... and Her Daughter, Persephone, Who Gave Us Winter

When she was out picking flowers one day, the young and beautiful Persephone was abducted by Hades, ruler of the Underworld. Distraught, Demeter came down from Olympus to find her daughter, and everything on Earth stopped growing. Too late—her daughter had eaten a pomegranate seed while she was in Hades' domain, and so was condemned to live there forever! Her father, the all-powerful Zeus, ruled that Persephone could return to live with her mother for six months of the year; her annual return to the surface heralds the coming of spring on Earth. During the other six months, which she must spend with Hades, all nature is still and winter descends on the land.

Figurine of Demeter

Her head covered, the goddess weeps for her lost daughter, Persephone. Produced in the famous workshops of ancient Tanagra. The head was broken and later repaired, apparently so that the figurine could still be used.

Olbia site, village of Paroutino, Nikolayev province (1995)
4th - 3rd century B.C.
Terracotta
Height 56 mm
IA NUAS, Inv. No. O-81/r-19/765

Bust of Corè*-Persephone

Her face and stance are so youthful looking that it's easy to forget that she is 2,300 years old! One of the best examples of Greek-era sculpture from the Black Sea region.
* "young girl," in Greek

Olbia site, village of Paroutino, Nikolayev province (1974)
3rd century B.C.
Terracotta
Height 282 mm
IA NUAS, Inv. No. O-74/S-3/116

"I have lost my Eurydice…

… my misery has no equal!", laments Orpheus in Gluck's famous opera, based on one of the most important Greek myths. Here the tale is represented on a magnificent low relief, produced in Olbia. It is the finest of its kind ever discovered.

....

Low relief representing Orpheus, Eurydice and Hermes
The scene depicts the fateful moment when Orpheus turns to look behind him. Hermes, the guide of souls, is leading the couple. The slightly rounded surface suggests that this may have been applied to a funerary urn.

Olbia site, village of Paroutino, Nikolayev province (1974)
Second half of 4th century B.C.
Terracotta
Dim. 170 x 150 x 10-15 mm
IA NUAS, Inv. No. O-74/UZA/500

The despair of Orpheus

Orpheus and Eurydice loved each other deeply. One day, as she was out walking, Eurydice encountered Aristaeus, who attempted to seduce her. As she fled his attentions, she was bitten by a serpent, and died. Orpheus, despairing, descended to the Kingdom of the Dead to beg Hades, ruler of the Underworld, to give him back his beloved. The god relented, but warned Orpheus that he must not look behind him to see whether she was following until they both emerged into the daylight.

But Orpheus forgot this command as soon as he reached the surface and turned to look behind him. He never saw Eurydice again.

....

Sculpture representing Artemis (facing page)
This magnificent sculpture, created in the workshops of ancient Alexandria, Egypt, is in the purest Hellenistic tradition. The artist has captured Artemis in full flight. On one side of the goddess' short, belted chiton, she wears a quiver for her arrows. The head, hands and feet were not found.

Olbia site, village of Paroutino, Nikolayev province (1970)
Late 3rd century - early 2nd century B.C.
Marble
Height 430 mm
IA NUAS, Inv. No. AM-1144/5253

Artemis, the Huntress

The Romans called Demeter's other daughter Diana. A fierce young maiden whose only passion was the hunt, she was worshipped as Artemis in the wild and mountainous areas of Greece. She was the protectress of the Amazons, who like her were female warriors and huntresses who bowed to no man. In fact, one of Herodotus' captivating tales recounts how they crossed paths with the Scythians in legend.

How the Scythians won the Amazons

The Greeks defeated the Amazons at the battle of Thermodon, and began taking them back as captives on their ships—but the Amazons revolted at sea and massacred the crew. Unfortunately, these seasoned warriors, whom the Scythians called *Oiorpata,* or "man killers," knew nothing of navigation, and drifted until they landed on the shores of Scythian territory.

There they captured a herd of wild horses and ravaged the countryside. The Scythians retaliated, and discovered to their astonishment when they began looting their slain opponents' bodies that their enemies were women! They changed tactics, sending a detachment of young men to befriend the invaders, in hopes of having children by them.

The two camps watched each other, without attacking, both of them living by hunting and plundering, until one day a Scythian came upon an Amazon by herself, and made advances to her. She did not resist, Herodotus says. Even better, she invited her companion to return the next day with a friend, promising to bring another Amazon with her. The rest of both camps soon followed suit.

The Scythian men, Herodotus adds, never managed to learn the Amazon language, whereas the Amazons quickly learned Scythian. They refused, however, to return home with the Scythians as their wives, much preferring to retain their independence. So, unlike their Scythian counterparts, who were confined to camp, the Amazons continued to hunt and fight and dress like men.

The story of the Amazons is a legend. But archaeological research has confirmed that in some nomad tribes, women rode to the hunt, fought in wars and served as leaders.

Figurine of a soldier

This soldier in a barbarian's garb (i.e. non-Greek), produced in a Greek colony on the Black Sea, stands with his left hand on his shield and his right hand on his chest, a pose that dates him to late antiquity. He was found in a location reserved for worship in a house.

Tiras site, town of Belgorod on the Dniestr, Odessa province (1958)
2nd - 3rd century A.D.
Stone
Height 194 mm
IA NUAS, Inv. No. BD-58/1189

On the Steppes, History Repeats Itself

The nomads' peaceful relations with their Greek neighbours lasted only so long. For other hordes of nomad warriors surged out of the South, the North and especially the East, with new waves rolling in turn over the steppes.

The Cimmerians, then the Scythians and the Sarmatians each had their day. Then came the Huns, led by Attila, later the Avars, then the Khazars, then the Pechenegs, and the Polovtsians…

Even after the artists decorated these clay eggs in the 12th century, new invaders and oppressors continued to thunder down on the fertile, black Ukrainian *chernozem*, or soil. Each wave brought its share of devastation and cultural contributions, all merging to form a country waiting to be born.

Painted eggs

The Ukrainian tradition of painted eggs—today associated with Easter, but linked to birth and fertility since time immemorial—is a very ancient practice. Remains of stone and clay eggs, albeit undecorated, have been found in tombs dating back to the Bronze Age. These are two of the oldest painted eggs ever discovered in Ukraine, about a dozen in all, in tombs dating from the 10th to 12th centuries.

Village of Voyinskaya Greblya, Cherkassy province (1985-1986)
12th century A.D.
Ceramic
Diam. 40-43 mm; height 58 mm; max. diam. 43 mm
IA NUAS, Inv. No. 1495, 1496

The Exhibition: An Overview

Ukraine Rediscovered: History and Archaeology

Véronique Schiltz, Archaeology Laboratory
of the École Normale Supérieure and the Université de France-Comté

This exhibition is absolutely exceptional in several respects. For the first time, the Institute of Archaeology of the National Ukrainian Academy of Sciences, in Kiev, is presenting its collections abroad. For the first time, the public has direct access, "live" access if you will, to the fruits of years of archaeological research on Ukrainian soil.

As can be seen as one wanders through the different sections, very well explained here by Elena Fialko and Denis Kozak, this research covers over twenty thousand years of history, stretching from the Paleolithic to late Antiquity. The age of the great steppe nomads of Antiquity, the Scythians, and their contacts with their Greek contemporaries on the shores of the Black Sea are particularly well illustrated.

In presenting the archaeology of Ukraine, it would naturally have been possible to make different choices; other pieces, some of them very prestigious ones, could have been exhibited. Many of them, today part of the collections of the Hermitage Museum in St. Petersburg or the Ukraine Historic Treasures Museum in Kiev, have in fact often been displayed before. They have travelled all over the world in recent years, and are now well known. But the interest of this exhibition lies precisely in its original selection, intended to show a different side of Ukrainian archaeology. By drawing on the riches housed in the Institute of Archaeology of the National Ukrainian Academy of Sciences, the exhibition focusses on Ukraine and pays tribute to the archaeologists who have laboured to reveal the secrets in its soil.

Some of these objects are indispensable everyday items, tools or weapons, others seemingly useless decorations, some of them made of humble bits of bone and others cast in the most sumptuous gold, but all hold equal wealth for those who know how to make them speak and to place them in context.

These treasures come from Ukraine, a very young state with its roots extending back to the dawn of time. But what does this concept of Ukraine mean for most visitors?

The Ukrainian identity

Even in Canada, where the Ukrainian community is particularly large and active, most people know little more than folk tales and some very appealing clichés. Images come to mind, of women with welcoming smiles wearing flowery crowns adorned with ribbons, marvellously embroidered peasant blouses, and multicoloured skirts and aprons. Then there are silhouettes of moustached Cossacks, their heads shaved or sporting tall fur hats, in boots and baggy pants, equally ready to raise their glasses or to seize their weapons and ride off into the fray… when they are not writing insulting letters to some Ottoman sultan. Of course, there are also the visions of endless wheat fields waving in the wind, or the euphoric photographs of years gone by, showing bright new combines bringing in a rich harvest, or miners with their goggles pushed up on their foreheads, grinning through the coal dust.

Historical figures come to mind as well—Mazepa, of course, but this has more to do with a romantic myth engendered by Pushkin, Byron and Victor Hugo than with Ukrainian history, and Delacroix's splendid image of a naked Mazepa lashed to a wild horse. And speaking of the Cossacks, and their struggle for independence, what do visitors know of Bogdan Khmelnytsky and his role in the liberation of Ukraine?

And in literature, we have Nikolay Gogol, or rather Mykola Hohol, the Ukrainian-born writer who penned his *Evenings on a Farm near Dikanka* and *Taras Bulba* in Russian. But what do non-Ukrainians know of Ukrainian literature? Have they read Lesya Ukrayinka, or even the great Taras Shevchenko?

The most suggestive image, and the most common, even in the minds of those who have not had the good fortune to see it in person, is doubtless the city of Kiev (which we should logically call by its Ukrainian name of Kyiv, incidentally). Kiev the superb, spilling down toward the Dniepr. Kiev the green, a southern city in its bright light and easy living. Kiev the Baroque, with its fantastic faces and masks, the multitude of animals adorning its facades and the living presence of its cats. Kiev the Medieval, with its many churches and the Byzantine splendour of the Cathedral of Saint Sophia and its golden domes. Kiev, the "mother of Rus cities."

This latter description of Kiev, attributed to Oleg, the first prince to have imposed his will on the city and the Dniepr basin, in the late 9th century, sums up all the ambiguity of the history of the capital city, and the paradox of Ukraine itself. For if Kiev is the mother of Rus cities, if Kievan Rus is the cradle of the Russian state, where is Ukraine? Indeed, until quite recently, Ukraine appeared on many maps and in many documents as "Little Russia" or "South Russia."

The confusion between Ukraine and Russia is real, and too often deliberately maintained in modern times. Ukraine is certainly something other than a Russian province, but what do we know, really, about a Ukrainian history too often seen from the point of view of the Imperial capital of St. Petersburg, or the Soviet capital of Moscow? The very name it calls itself, "Ukraine," is paradoxical and ambiguous. "Ukraina" means the frontier, the border-land, the marches, the periphery. Who could have named it thus if not outsiders, covetous external powers who saw themselves as the centre? Ruled by absent landlords, suppressed, occupied and sometimes divided up, this was the difficult destiny of a Ukraine that was constantly in thrall to foreign powers and spent centuries coming into its own.

Digging into the past

Let us proceed as archaeologists do, from the top down, beginning with the modern age and studying the visible surface, the most recent layer, before digging down through successive strata into the past. In 1991, the Ukrainian Republic regained its lost freedom. Independence was declared on August 24, and approved in a popular referendum on December 1 by all the inhabitants of Ukrainian territory, regardless of nationality. Never before had Ukraine been allowed to exist as a full-fledged state. With a brief interlude when the independent Ukrainian Republic emerged immediately after the 1917 revolution, Ukraine joined the vast Soviet Union in 1922, merely picking up where its membership in the Russian empire had left off. Its role in that respect had begun in the mid-17th century, when the Cossack Ukrainian state was annexed to Russia, and was then energetically confirmed in the late 18th century by Catherine the Great, who extended Russian domination all the way to the shores of the Black Sea.

In reality, after the fall of Kiev, sacked in 1240 by the Mongol Tatars, just as a truly Ukrainian identity was beginning to emerge, the territory of present-day Ukraine was constantly fought over by covetous neighbours, the Grand Duchy of Lithuania, then Poland, while its shores, first in the hands of the Nogai Tatars, passed into the hands of the Ottoman Empire and the Crimean khan after 1475.

One last layer to consider before we arrive in antiquity: the Kievan state that enjoyed such splendour in the 11th and 12th centuries. How should we define it? Was it truly Russian? Can we consider it even at that far-off time as Ukrainian? Formulated in this way, the question is actually misleading; we must ask it in different terms.

When Prince Oleg, son of Rurik, arrived from Novgorod at the end of the 9th century to impose his power on the Dniepr Basin and the Kiev region, he was simply following the "Road from the Varangians to the Greeks," a trade route along the rivers between the Baltic and the Mediterranean. This water road had been travelled ever since the 8th century, as Arab coins found far to the north, near Lake Ladoga, attest, and could be followed south-ward via the Don and the Sea of Azov. But the shortest itinerary, and especially the safest, in that it was less exposed to attacks by nomads from the Asian steppes, was the route along the Dniepr leading directly to the Black Sea.

It is not surprising, then, that Oleg took a great interest in the land around the Dniepr and, on its right bank, the site of Kiev, with its port on the river and its easily defended heights. But like Rurik before him, like Prince Igor, and after him like Queen Olga, grandmother of Prince Vladimir, who baptized his people in the Dniepr in 988, Oleg was a Varangian, a Scandinavian. When he arrived at the site of Kiev, he found—and archaeologists have since confirmed—a city that already boasted a long history. At this site, and even more in the surrounding territory, there were West Slavs, Scandinavian Varangians, and Polyanes from the wooded steppes. It is not by chance that legend attributes the founding of the city to Kiy and his two brothers, who were neither Slavs nor Varangians, but rather members of the steppes tribe known as Polyanes.

This ancient Russia, which it would be better to refer to as Rus, to avoid ambiguity, was neither Russian nor Ukrainian. It was already a thorough ethnic mixture. No one people can claim it for its own. Any other view is merely hindsight, prompted by a geopolitical vision that has much more to do with present ambitions than past realities.

Considering the State of Kiev to be the birthplace of Russia is potentially doubly misleading. For on the one hand, the history of Russia does not begin with Kiev, but before, and much farther north. On the other hand, if indeed there was a cradle, it was common to all the West Slavs, who very soon mixed with other peoples. In terms of the history of peoples, the idea of a single founding people is almost invariably a myth. On the soil of what is now Ukraine, the Slavs were newcomers who mingled with those who were already there—as the Sarmatians had done in their time, and the Scythians before them.

The existence, in a young Ukrainian state, of a national (but not nationalist) archaeology should allow us to take a more considered view of these questions of the historic roots and ethnogenesis of the different peoples. We can only hope that the days have forever disappeared when, as in the Stalinist period, an archaeologist remotely controlled from Moscow could fearlessly claim that "proto-slavs" had always, or almost always, inhabited both Ukraine and Russia and Central Europe.

Archaeologists' labours

This exhibition shows that our Ukrainian archaeologist colleagues are well aware that the wealth of their homeland, their nation, stems from these fertile mixtures. The Ukrainian identity has been forged from many different ores. It is none the less real, and the Ukrainian state, at once very young and very old, is determined to reclaim its past in all its diversity.

Digs in Ukraine are part of a very long tradition. It was on the right-hand bank of the Dniepr, starting in 1763, that a Scythian kurgan was systematically excavated for the first time. The work was carried out briskly by soldiers; their commander, General Melgunov, who had initiated the digs, did not even see fit to accompany them. Although it could not exactly be termed a pillage, no one thought to record the layout of the tomb and the location of the different items. The objects recovered, a sword with a gold-plated handle and scabbard, a diadem and seventeen small eagle-shaped gold plaques, were dispatched to the commander of a Russian fortress nearby, and then presented to Her Imperial Majesty Catherine II, in St. Petersburg. She had them placed in the *Kunstkamera*, the curiosity cabinet created at the beginning of the century by Peter the Great, and which already held a collection of ancient golden artifacts unearthed in Siberia.

And so began, for Ukraine, a tradition that diverted the most splendid finds in the Russian Empire to St. Petersburg, the capital. This practice persisted until 1917, so much so that even today many of the prime pieces recovered from Ukrainian soil can be seen only in the Hermitage Museum. Our exhibition is, after a fashion, a counterweight to this over-centralization that has deprived Ukraine of many of its treasures. And treasures there were in plenty, for starting in the late 18th century, after the Turks were driven from the shores of the Black Sea, the mouth of the Dniepr and the Crimea, and even more in the first third of the 19th century, the number of finds grew by leaps and bounds. In 1859, a Russian Imperial Archaeological Commission was founded, marking the birth of a scientific approach to archaeology—official archaeology, at least, for amateur digs and grave robbing remained very common. It was not until the digs at Kul' Oba, in 1830, that the face of these mysterious Scythians, previously known only through literature, was finally revealed, modelled on a golden vessel. This brought them new life in the literature of the time, as well. By a not-so-strange coincidence, the young John Ruskin, before becoming the apostle of modern art and well-known architectural authority, wrote of their tombs, their music and their customs ("The Scythian grave," 1838; "A Scythian banquet song," 1839; "The Scythian guest," 1849).

The most sensational archaeological discovery was doubtless the undisturbed tomb beneath the Solokha kurgan, in 1913: it revealed horses and servants, abundant dishes, weapons and jewellery (today in the Hermitage Museum); even the layout of the tomb confirmed the account by the Greek historian Herodotus of the funeral rites of Scythian kings. Perhaps inspired by this spectacular find, Sergey Prokofiev composed his "Scythian Suite" in 1914.

Following the disruption of World War I and the 1917 revolution, Lenin signed the decree founding the Russian Academy of the History of Material Culture in 1919. This was the successor to the Imperial Archaeological Commission and, in 1937, became the Institute of Archaeology of the USSR Academy of Sciences. It was headquartered in Moscow, but had local sections, including one in Kiev. Digs were carried out jointly by Russian archaeologists and their Ukrainian colleagues. Rather than exploring the richest kurgans, they focussed on different aspects, even the most humble, of "material culture." In addition, growing urbanization and major civil works (irrigation and farming on the steppes, construction of the Kakhovka dam upstream of the Dniepr rapids) led to new research. At the same time, kurgans that had been excavated earlier were studied again, yielding a new harvest of information and pieces. This was the case for the silver vessel found in 1985 at Chertomlyk, more than a century after the first digs there, and presented in this exhibition; and of the objects rediscovered in 1980-1981 in the Oguz kurgan, which had in fact been explored early this century.

Archaeologists in Ukraine have been particularly busy in recent decades and are struggling to continue their work despite difficulties linked to the emergence of a market economy with little sympathy for activities that show no immediate profit. There is no doubt that the soil of Ukraine still hides abundant riches. All these finds are of equal scientific interest, but some of them may also offer the glittering seduction of gold—some of the royal kurgans that remain to be searched, or re-searched, surely still contain true treasures. Our Ukrainian colleagues must have the resources to undertake this work, however. For many of them, these resources are cruelly lacking, and the situation is becoming critical. If we do not lend our help to Ukrainian archaeology it may be condemned to futility, just when it has proven its merits. This exhibition could also provide an opportunity for fruitful meetings and lay the groundwork for great plans.

There are many ways to explore this exhibition. Both the physical exhibition and the catalogue have been designed to be accessible to all visitors and attractive to the eye. The beholder needs no prior knowledge to be able to enjoy the experience.

A walk through the exhibition

The full-figured statuettes from the Tripolye civilization, the strength flowing through the Scythian images of stags and horses, the immediate familiarity of a bronze cauldron and its ladle reach out to the viewer, while the precious golden Scythian vessels and the refinement and abundance of jewellery are unfailingly seductive.

Visitors can also allow themselves to be carried away by the emotional experience of seeing objects that in some cases—the splendid gold-plated silver vessel from Soboleva Mogila for instance—were until quite recently buried deep in the earth. Running one's eyes over these magnificent pieces, one can almost instantly feel the centuries melt away and share the feelings of the craftsmen who created them, the men and women who handled them or placed them carefully next to their loved ones to speed them on their way to the next world.

Those who found delight in the company of Greek gods and goddesses in their youth will be pleased to encounter the giants of classical mythology again: Heracles, Medusa the Gorgon, Demeter and her daughter Persephone, and Orpheus who lost his beloved Eurydice.

In short, the exhibition has something for everyone. Allow me to offer a few comments on some of the highlights.

The exhibition opens with the Paleolithic Mezine site and the remains of a young mammoth. Its presence illustrates both the most modern analytical techniques and the most archaic thought processes. Thanks to advances in new fields of scientific analysis, the traces left by man and his tools on the surface of the bone can be deciphered with ease, and we can even "read" the motions of the craftsman's hand: what tools were used, how the blows were delivered, in what order, with what hesitations and what corrections. But beyond what these traces tell us of the technical skills of Homo sapiens and his possible enjoyment of rhythmic music, these mammoth bones also evoke the passage from myth to History, and the beginnings of a transition from a view of the past still rooted in the Holy Scriptures. For when the remains of mammoths were first found in the 18th century, they were thought to be from elephants drowned in the great Flood and left behind as the waters receded!

The clay-covered human skull dating from the early 2nd millennium B.C., from a kurgan in Zaporozhye province, tells us how the steppe dwellers attached particular importance to conserving skulls. They treated them in different ways: either by taking positive steps, as we see here, to preserve the image of the deceased and assure him a form of survival; or by making use of the skull in a practice that likely had more to do with magic than vengeance. Herodotus tells how the skulls of enemies were carefully cut open and lined with rawhide and, for wealthier warriors, gilded on the inside, to serve as drinking cups. Well-documented archaeological finds have confirmed this practice in Scythian times. One cannot help but think of the beginnings of the Kievan state, and how in 972, the Pecheneg chief Kouria ordered that Svyatoslav (the first prince of Kiev to bear a Slavonic name rather than a Varangian one) be beheaded and his skull made into a silver-lined drinking cup.

The many harness trappings, too, are very striking, from the bits and bit bars of the Cimmerian epoch to the various frontlets, nose guards, cheek guards and pendants of bronze, silver and gold found in 4th-century kurgans, illustrating the essential role of the horse in life on the steppes. Indeed, the horse was as important to the nomads as the boat was to the Greeks. And Cicero's anecdote of a Scythian shepherd who was amazed to see a ship moving on the water is merely a reflection of this deep symmetry between two modes of transportation—between sailing through waves of water on the sea and riding through waves of grasses on land. The omnipresence of horses and their equipment in nomads' tombs is such that harness trappings, along with weapons and the animal style, constitute the Scythian "triad" used to identify Scythian-type archaeological cultures. Far from contenting themselves with merely inventing trousers, the saddle, spurs and stirrups, these horsemen who lived by the wind and the sword were largely responsible for laying the original foundations of western European societies, and hence our own.

These horsemen, after all, quickly evolved into knights. The institution of chivalry as it developed in the Middle Ages, its heraldic vocabulary and many of its insignia, not to mention the sport of falconry, originated on the steppes.

In Ukraine itself, the groups of Cossacks that sprang up in the 15th century and were to play a decisive role in the history of the country had much in common with the nomads of antiquity. Of course, this bond is not a genetic link—in any case, how would one define a Cossack ethnic group? Rather, they shared a way of life, that of highly mobile horsemen with some home bases. Both remained near the lower course of the Dniepr, on the Kamenskoye site for the Scythians and, for the Cossacks, downstream of the cataracts.

This area, where the Dniepr crossed the successive rocky "steps" that made navigation impossible, stretched for about 75 km to the south of where Dniepropetrovsk now stands. Today immersed beneath the waters of the Kakhovka dam, the area was once very impressive, to judge by the 10th-century description by the Byzantine Emperor Constantine Pophyrogenitus. Farther downstream, the lazier Dniepr split into many arms, embracing islands rich with greenery and game. This is where the fortress of the famous Zaporozhian Cossacks was located in the 16th-18th centuries, their capital in a way, before Catherine the Great of Russia had it savagely razed by Potemkin in 1775, following the revolt by the Cossack Pugachov. But the closest bonds between the Cossacks and their predecessors on the steppes lies above all in their shared rejection of oppression in any form, their shared love of freedom and the values that go with it. This philosophy is still very much alive in today's Ukraine, once again doubtless thanks to the Cossacks.

Finally, we must also speak of the objects in this exhibition from the Olbia site. They illustrate the presence of the Greeks at the mouth of the Dniepr and on the shores of the Black Sea, and the contacts that developed there between the civilization that we call "classical" and those other cultures that—as did the Greeks—we tend to think of as "barbarian." There is much to say about and many lessons to be learned from this meeting of two worlds so very different that they might have been condemned to ignore or even fight one another.

We can see the admirably fertile results of their contact in the evidence presented here, and particularly in one of the major pieces in the exhibition: the golden phiale decorated with horses, discovered in 1990 in the Bratolubovsky kurgan. The six forequarters of the horses on its base are in the finest Greek style, equal in every way to the rearing horses on the Parthenon frieze. Doubtless a Greek goldsmith, or one trained by the Greeks, fashioned this piece. Yet an artist from Athens could never have produced such a delight all by himself. The shape of the object, naturally, the gold from which it is made and the haunting image of these six carefully harnessed heads alone are enough to indicate the Scythian influence. But even more, the nomad's mark can be seen in the lack of a frame, the refusal to be shut in, as the image appears to be escaping its background. The whirling and spinning design seems to suggest perpetual motion, confusing the sedentary regard that seeks a fixed frame, a top and bottom, a beginning and end. In short, these fluid forms are pure motion, transforming space into movement.

What we have here goes far beyond what is often called, with some measure of disdain, "Scythian taste." This Greco-Scythian piece represents a sort of bilingualism, the very essence of the nomad existence and the vital need to claim for one's own an open space as unlimited as the vast steppes.

The principal lesson it offers us is this: art is more than a simple reflection of the society that produces it. Rather, art is what reconciles that society with the world around it and its lifestyle. In the end, art is what allows us to survive.

List of Other Pieces Exhibited

In the Stone Age

Bracelet fragments
Dwelling No. 1, Mezine camp, Chernigov province (1954)
15,000 B.C.
Mammoth ivory, wolf or fox bone
Length 25-51 mm; width 10-17 mm; thickness 2 mm
IA NUAS, Inv. No. AM-2324/6534-6538

In the Time of the Tripolye People

Double vessel
Village of Chkarovka, Kiev province (1973)
3,250 – 2,900 B.C.
Clay
Height 190 mm; length 300 mm; width 141 mm
IA NUAS, Inv. No. AM 2325/6529

Double vessel, connected
Village of Rossokhvatka, Cherkassy province (1970)
3,250 – 2,900 B.C.
Clay
Height 55 mm; length 145 mm; width 80 mm
IA NUAS, Inv. No. AM 280/1217

Model of a dwelling, perhaps for cultic purposes
Village of Rossokhvatka, Cherkassy province (1970)
3,250 – 2,900 B.C.
Clay
Height 255 mm; length 295 mm; width 185 mm
IA NUAS, Inv. No. AM 281/1218

Platter decorated with a cross
Village of Bernachevka, Vinnitsa province (1989, 1990)
3,000 – 2,900 B.C.
Clay
Height 70 mm; diam. 185 mm
IA NUAS, Inv. No. AM 2251/6397

Platter decorated with a snake motif
Village of Bernachevka, Vinnitsa province (1989, 1990)
3,000 – 2,900 B.C.
Clay
Height 75 mm; diam. 160 mm
IA NUAS, Inv. No. AM 2244/6389

Fragment of an anthropomorphic figurine
Village of Bernachevka, Vinnitsa province (1989, 1993)
3,000 – 2,600 B.C.
Clay
Length 100 mm
IA NUAS, Inv. No. AM 2248/6394

Fragment of an anthropomorphic figurine
Village of Pavolotch, Zhitomir province (1947)
3,000 - 2600 B.C.
Clay
Height 45 mm
IA NUAS, Inv. No. AM 2164/6242

Bear figurine
Village of Kossenovka, Cherkassy province (1988)
3,100 – 2,850 B.C.
Clay
Height 100 mm; length 145 mm; width 85 mm

Duck's-head rattle
Village of Grebeni, Kiev province (1961)
3,100 – 2,850 B.C.
Clay
Height 45 mm; length 55 mm; width 32 mm
IA NUAS, Inv. No. AM 241/1144

Zoomorphic vessel
Village of Grebeni, Kiev province (1962)
3,250 – 2,800 B.C.
Clay
Height 75 mm; length 150 mm; width 105 mm
IA NUAS, Inv. No. AM 233/1135

Model of an animal-shaped altar
Village of Berezovka, Kirovograd province (1991)
3,250 – 2,800 B.C.
Height 75 mm; diam. 180 mm
IA NUAS, Inv. No. AM 2218/6357

Platter in the form of a sled
Village of Talianki, Cherkassy province (1984)
3,250 – 2,800 B.C.
Height 110 mm; length 130 mm; width 105 mm
Clay

In the Bronze Age

Stone hammer
Kurgan, village of Petro-Mikhaylovka, Zaporozhye province (1981)
20th-18th – 16th-10th century B.C.
Granite
Dim. 82 x 41 mm; diam. opening 16 mm
IA NUAS, Inv. No. 916

In the Time of the Cimmerians

Bit with bit attachments
Kurgan, village of Olchany, Cherkassy province (1984)
Second half 8th century - early 7th century B.C.
Bronze
Length 292 mm
IA NUAS, Inv. No. 680

Bit bars, or psalia
Kurgan No. 1, village of Zolnoye, near Simferopol, Crimea (1959)
Second half 8th century - early 7th century B.C.
Bronze
Length 140/142 mm
IA NUAS, Inv. No. 59/60

In the Time of the Scythians

Harness trappings, many showing evidence of deliberate blows on the back
Soboleva Mogila site, village of Gorniatskoye, Dniepropetrovsk province (1990-1991)
4th century B.C.
Silver, bronze, iron
IA NUAS, Inv. No. KP-VI-662

Harness ornament showing Heracles as a young man
Babina Mogila site, village of Tarasso-Grigorievka, Dniepropetrovsk province (1986)
4th century B.C.
Silver, gold
Diam. 75 mm
IA NUAS, Inv. No. KP-IV-385

Necklace of double flowers
Oguz kurgan, village of Nizhnye Serogozy, Kherson province (1980-1981)
Late third quarter of 4th century B.C.
Gold
Diam. of rosettes 10 mm; weight 31.97 g
IA NUAS, Inv. No. Z-845-878

Earring in the shape of a seated sphinx
Oguz kurgan, village of Nizhnye Serogozy, Kherson province (1980-1981)
Late third quarter of 4th century B.C.
Gold
Dim. 35 x 11 mm; weight 6.52 g
IA NUAS, Inv. No. Z-462

Necklace of 84 balls with double points and 34 double flowers; in the centre of the necklace is the head of a woman
Oguz kurgan, village of Nizhnye Serogozy, Kherson province (1980-1981)
Late third quarter of 4th century B.C.
Gold
Length 440 mm; weight 21.04 g
IA NUAS, Inv. No. Z-891-1009

Torque with open ends
Kurgan No. 3, village of Chelugui, Zaporozhye province (1987)
4th century B.C.
Gold
Max. diam 260 mm; Min. diam. 100-120 mm; weight 263.6 g
IA NUAS, Inv. No. KP-IV-381

Man's necklace with lion-shaped tips
Soboleva Mogila site, village of Gorniatskoye, Dniepropetrovsk province (1990-1991)
4th century B.C.
Gold
Dim. 190 x 170 mm; weight 520.4 g
IA NUAS, Inv. No. Z-1825

Earring
Soboleva Mogila site, village of Gorniatskoye, Dniepropetrovsk province (1990-1991)
4th century B.C.
Gold
Dim. 39 x 35 mm; weight 9.01 g
IA NUAS, Inv. No. Z-1828

Ring with smooth plaque
Soboleva Mogila site, village of Gorniatskoye, Dniepropetrovsk province (1990-1991)
4th century B.C.
Gold
Dim. 23.5 x 23 mm; weight 16.8 g
IA NUAS, Inv. No. Z-1827

Ring with decorated plaque
Soboleva Mogiła site, village of Gorniatskoye,
Dniepropetrovsk province (1990-1991)
4th century B.C.
Gold
Dim. 27.2 x 14 mm; weight 25.8 g
IA NUAS, Inv. No. Z-1826

Ornament with sphinx, to be used on a head-dress
Kurgan No. 9, village of Malaya Lepetikha, Kherson province (1992)
4th century B.C.
Gold
Dim. and weight sphinx (11x): 37 x 5 mm, 29.89 g
IA NUAS, Inv. No. KP-703/1-2

Woman's robe with gold plaques (reconstruction)
Kurgan No. 1, town of Kamenka on the Dniepr,
Zaporozhye province (1986);
4th century B.C.
Dim. 7-17 mm; weight 6.84-11.76 g
IA NUAS, Inv. No. Z-231-245, 247-295

Conical head-dress with trains decorated with 243 plaques (reconstruction)
Tatianina Mogila site, town of Ordzhonikidze,
Dniepropetrovsk province (1986)
Mid-4th century B.C.
Gold
Dim. 15-25 mm; weight 7.21-49.69 g
IA NUAS, Inv. No. Z-1204, 1210, 1214-15, 1218, 1222-24, 1226-27, 1237, 1242-43, 1245, 1248-50, 1253, 1255-59, 1261, 1265, 1268, 1274, 1279-1280, 1283, 1289-1419, 1421-1503

Smooth rings (2)
Kurgan No. 1, town of Kamenka on the Dniepr,
Zaporozhye province (1986);
4th century B.C.
Gold
Diam. 17 mm; weight 2.58 g, 2.95 g
IA NUAS, Inv. No. Z-355, 357

Gorgons'- head plaques (2)
Kurgan No. 1, village of Vodoslavka, Kherson province (1983)
4th century B.C.
Gold
Diam. 24-25 mm
IA NUAS, Inv. No. Z-2262-2263

Replica of the Tolstaya Mogila pectoral
Plated copy
Diam. 306 mm
IA NUAS, Inv. No. NV-79

Decorated vessel
Soboleva Mogila site, village of Gorniatskoye,
Dniepropetrovsk province (1991-1992)
4th century B.C.
Gold-plated silver
Height 91 mm; diam. 86 mm
IA NUAS, Inv. No. KP-V-661

Wine goblet, or kilik
Soboleva Mogila site, village of Gorniatskoye,
Dniepropetrovsk province (1991-1992)
4th century B.C.
Silver
Height 50 mm; diam. 50 mm
IA NUAS, Inv. No. KP-V-670

Wine goblet
Chertomlyk kurgan, town of Nikopol,
Dniepropetrovsk province (1968-1972)
4th century B.C.
Silver
Height 155 mm; diam. 66 mm; weight 255.1 g
IA NUAS, Inv. No. KP-453

In the Time of the Sarmatians

Two-edged swords (2)
Kurgans of the Akkermen-II group, settlement of Novo Fillipovka,
Zaporozhye province (1952)
1st - 2nd century A.D.
Iron
Length 435 mm, width 33 mm; length 454 mm, width 53 mm
IA NUAS, Inv. No. 1081-1082

Arrowheads (5)
Tomb No. 1, kurgan of the Akkermen-II group,
settlement of Novo Fillipovka, Zaporozhye province (1952)
Second half 1st century A.D.
Iron
Length 22-27 mm
IA NUAS, Inv. No. 1083-1086

Mirror-pendant
Kurgan No. 8, Akkermen-II group, settlement of Novo Fillipovka,
Zaporozhye province (1952)
Second half 1st century A.D.
Bronze
Diam. disk 79 mm; length handle 30 mm
IA NUAS, Inv. No. 884

Mirror-pendant
Second half - late 2nd century A.D.
Tomb No. 1, kurgan No. 11, Akkermen-II group,
settlement of Novo Fillipovka, Zaporozhye province (1952)
Second half 1st century - late 2nd century A.D.
Bronze
Diam. disk 48 mm; length handle 11 mm
IA NUAS, Inv. No. 885

Fibula, of Roman origin
Settlement of Fedorovka, Zaporozhye province (1950)
1st century A.D.
Bronze
Length 64 mm; width of back 10 mm

Necklace
Settlement of Tolstoye, Ternopol province (1977)
1st century A.D.
Rock crystal, amethyst, carnelian, agate, amber, glass
Length 15-20 mm; diam. 8-12 mm

Necklace
Tomb No. 4, kurgan No. 3, settlement of Mayorovka,
Nikolayev province (1971); 1st century A.D.
Egyptian faience, glass, gold
Diam. 7-8 mm

On the Shores of the Black Sea

Mug, or modiolus
Olbia site, village of Paroutino, Nikolayev province (1983)
1st - 4th century A.D.
Glass
Height 134 mm; diam. top 136 mm
IA NUAS, Inv. No. Am-1161/5333

Guttus, with spout
Olbia site, village of Paroutino, Nikolayev province (1972)
1st - 4th century A.D.
Glass
Height 66-71 mm; diam. top 43-45 mm
IA NUAS, Inv. No. O-72/83

Container for balm
Olbia site, village of Paroutino, Nikolayev province (1983)
1st - 4th century A.D.
Glass
Height 96-100 mm; diam. top 47 mm
IA NUAS, Inv. No. O-83/Necr./397

Glass
Necropolis, village of Zamorskoye, Crimea (1967)
1st - 4th century A.D.
Glass
Height 65-68 mm; diam. top 60 mm
IA NUAS, Inv. No. Zamor.-67/115

Jug – possibly a perfume bottle
Necropolis, village of Zamorskoye, Crimea (1967)
1st - 4th century A.D.
Glass
Height 120-122 mm; diam. top 48 mm
IA NUAS, Inv. No. Zamor.-67/46

Head of Aphrodite, probably from the workshops of ancient Alexandria, in Egypt
Olbia site, village of Paroutino, Nikolayev province (1996)
3rd century B.C.
Marble
Height 106 mm
IA NUAS, Inv. No. O-96/r-25/500

Head of Aphrodite, from Syria
Berezan island site, Nikolayev province (1995)
4th - 3rd century B.C.
Terracotta
Height 62 mm
IA NUAS, Inv. No. AB-76

Mirror
Repiakhovataya Mogila site, village of Matoussov,
Cherkassy province (1974)
6th-4th century B.C.
Bronze, iron
Diam. disk 100 mm; handle 92 x 18 mm
IA NUAS, Inv. No. SSE-74, No 48

Amphora-shaped bottle for perfume or oil
Olbia site, village of Paroutino, Nikolayev province (1992)
5th century B.C.
Glass paste
Height 115 mm
IA NUAS, Inv. No. O-92/Necr./78

Pyxides – little covered flat-bottomed jars, used mainly for white and red make-up (2)
Olbia site, village of Paroutino, Nikolayev province (1985)
1st - 2nd century A.D.
Ivory
Height 33 mm, 40 mm
IA NUAS, Inv. No. O-85/Necr./176, 177

Belt buckle
Olbia site, village of Paroutino, Nikolayev province (1995)
4th century B.C.
Bronze
Length 42 mm, diam. tongue 3.5 mm
IA NUAS, Inv. No. O-95/Necr.Ch.B./P.2

Printed at Interglobe, Beauceville, Quebec.